JEWISH WASHINGTON:
SCRAPBOOK OF AN AMERICAN COMMUNITY

Laura Cohen Apelbaum and Wendy Turman, Editors

JEWISH HISTORICAL SOCIETY OF GREATER WASHINGTON

LILLIAN AND ALBERT SMALL JEWISH MUSEUM, WASHINGTON, DC

For over 40 years, the Jewish Historical Society of Greater Washington and its Lillian & Albert Small Jewish Museum have been chronicling the story of the Jewish community in Washington, D.C., and the suburbs of Maryland and Northern Virginia.

In 1969, the Society galvanized the community to preserve the historic 1876 Adas Israel Synagogue – the oldest in the Washington area – from demolition by moving it three city blocks to its current location at the corner of 3rd and G Streets, NW. After extensive renovation and restoration, the synagogue was rededicated and opened to the public as the Lillian and Albert Small Jewish Museum. The synagogue is listed on the National Register of Historic Places, the DC Inventory of Historic Sites, the Historic American Buildings Survey, and it is an Official Project of Save America's Treasures.

The Society maintains the only community-wide archive of the local Jewish community. The collections include personal papers, organizational records, and over 1,800 photographs which trace the history of the Jewish community from the mid-19th century through the present day. The Society houses over 100 oral histories from longtime members and leaders of the local Jewish community. Public programming includes walking tours, lectures, and book talks. Over 1,000 school children participate in annual educational field trips and view living history performances.

The Society also publishes THE RECORD, a journal about local Jewish history. For more than twenty years, the Jewish Historical Society has mounted exhibits based on original research that have traveled throughout the metropolitan area. The Society is a local leader in the concept of "public space Judaism," mounting exhibits and programs in venues accessible and welcoming to the greater public.

Copyright 2007

Jewish Historical Society of Greater Washington
Lillian and Albert Small Jewish Museum
701 4th Street, N.W. Washington, D.C. 20001

202.789.0900   info@jhsgw.org   www.jhsgw.org

Laura Cohen Apelbaum and Wendy Turman, editors

First Edition

Designed by Jeanne Krohn Design   Printed in China by Hong Kong Graphics & Printing, Ltd. on Archival Paper.

ISBN 978-0-9792365-0-1

Library of Congress Control Number: 2007921698

Cover:
Flagraising ceremony at Washington Hebrew Congregation, 1917. JHSGW Collections.

Inside front cover:
Rosh Hashanah card, ca. 1910. JHSGW Collections. Gift of Edith and Charles Pascal.

Page IV:
District Grocery Store banquet, 1927. JHSGW Collections. Gift of Barbara Rein. 1989.08

JEWISH WASHINGTON:
SCRAPBOOK OF AN AMERICAN COMMUNITY

The following individuals and organizations
generously contributed to make the publication of this book possible:

FOLIO LEVEL

Sulica Fund

United Jewish Endowment Fund of
The Jewish Federation of Greater Washington

Barbara & Bert Rein

The Doris & Robert I. Silverman Endowment Fund

Albert H. Small

The Albert & Lillian Small Foundation

The Small-Alper Family Foundation

The Charles E. Smith Family Foundation

Nancy & Carl Gewirz

The Jacob & Charlotte Lehrman Foundation

The Povich Family

SECTION LEVEL

The Henry & Ann Reich Family Foundation

The Jonathan S. & Patricia G. England Family Foundation

PARAGRAPH LEVEL

Lois & Richard England

SENTENCE LEVEL

Abramson Family Foundation	Barbara & Jack Kay
Joy & Bruce Ammerman	Paula Pascal Levine
The Bender Foundation	Irene & Abe Pollin
Martha & Stuart Bindeman	Tina & Albert Small, Jr.
The Giant Food Foundation	Michael Towbes

WORD LEVEL

Howard Schreier	Ann & Frank Gilbert	Saul Stern
Josephine Ammerman	The Hon. & Mrs. Joseph Gildenhorn	Hadassah Thursz
Flora & Maury Atkin	Paula Goldman	Diane Abelman Wattenberg
The Hon. & Mrs. Stuart Bernstein	Monica & Hermen Greenberg	Carole & Joseph Wolinsky
Linda & Richard Blumenreich	Foundation	Mendelle T. & Jack Woodley
Rebecca & David Burka	Judith & Michael Herman	
Frances & Leonard Burka	Jeannette Kressin	and Joan & Oscar Dodek, Corinne & Martin
Maria & Robert Burka	Betty Lichtenstein	Kamerow, Helen & Norman Kamerow, Evelyn
Funger Foundation	Ralph Ochsman	Sacks, Dr. and Mrs. William Binder, Louis &
Martin Garfinkle	Myrna Sislen & Bill Rice	Dorothy Kornhauser, Gary Malasky, Robin &
	Roberta & Charles Sonneborn	Karmi Leiman, Betty Kamerow, Anadel & Frank
		Rich, and Rhoda & Nelson Marans

TABLE OF CONTENTS

FOREWORD

The story of Washington's Jewish community is often told only as a simple time-line. Jews came "late" to the city, followed the "usual" patterns of immigration, opened small shops that grew into large stores, organized synagogues and Jewish communal organizations, and then moved out to the suburbs.

This book, which began as a landmark exhibition, adds depth and dimension to the story. Drawing on our rich community archives, the Jewish Historical Society of Greater Washington created the exhibition to honor the 350th anniversary of Jewish life in America. Titled *Jewish Washington: Scrapbook of An American Community,* it opened on June 23, 2005, at the National Building Museum, and attracted unprecedented attendance and media attention. The exhibition's wealth of images, many never before seen by the public, depict a Washington that is both the nation's capital and hometown to the sixth largest Jewish community in the United States.

We were honored to receive a 2006 Leadership in History Award of Merit from the American Association of State and Local History (AASLH) for the exhibition. Since 1945, this has been the most prestigious recognition for achievement in the preservation and interpretation of state and local history.

We invite you to turn these pages where you will find a chronicle of the day-to-day lives and deeds of community members. Many of the images come from the Society's collection of more than fifty scrapbooks, each lovingly filled with newspaper clippings, dried corsages, invitations, and photographs of the people, places, and events that illustrate our community's dynamic development. The format of this book and hence its title fittingly take their cue from this valuable, if informal, record of our community's unique history and its role in American Jewish life and the nation's history. These materials, and the rest of the Society's collections, form the nation's central archives for this special community and are open to the public for research.

Jews were "late" in arriving in the nation's capital, simply because there was no town or city in which to settle before 1800, when the federal government moved into the rural, swampy, newly created District of Columbia. By that time, New York, Boston, Philadelphia, and Charleston were well-established colonial cities with substantial Jewish populations. Our research shows that the first Jew to settle in Washington arrived in 1795. Other Jews followed, and after 1840, a wave of immigration began that, during the 19th and 20th centuries, brought tens of thousands of Jewish immigrants to this city. Jews from Central Europe arrived first, followed by those from Eastern Europe and Russia, with Sephardic Jews settling here in the 1920s.

While many started in business with small shops—groceries, furniture stores, tailors, jewelers—the presence of the federal government had a profound effect. Stores' clientele included presidents, Supreme Court justices and members of Congress. The few Jews who served in the federal government for the century preceding the New Deal were joined by a wave of young intellectuals who arrived to serve a burgeoning federal government in the 1930s and 1940s. Continued growth and prosperity since World War II have created a metropolitan area that spans three jurisdictions—the District of Columbia and the Maryland and Northern Virginia suburbs—that include more than 215,000 members.

Creation of this book depended heavily on the help and advice of some very special people. Many are acknowledged in its pages. Several warrant special mention here. Frank B. Gilbert and Peggy Pearlstein served as presidents during the long process of conceiving and financing its publication. Ann Belkov provided constant encouragement, as did Patrick Gallagher. Dr. Pamela Nadell of American University and Dr. Hasia Diner of New York University were instrumental in reviewing our text and making suggestions for historical accuracy. Sharon L. Barry helped refine the words to convey the stories we wanted to tell, and Gail Spilsbury and Dr. Laura Burd Schiavo laid the groundwork for publication. We relied on Nathalie Lavine, Claire Uziel, and Amy Federman on the Society's staff to help pull together many aspects of the book. Joel Wind, Stephanie Silverstein, and Diane Goldman provided support especially in marketing this book. Jeanne Krohn of Krohn Design created a design that so beautifully and perfectly reflected our collections and our work. She was a true partner in every step of the production.

The impetus for the exhibition and book came from a discussion Dr. Gary Zola, Director of the American Jewish Archives, led at a conference of the Council of American Jewish Museums in Cincinnati in early 2002. Dr. Zola spoke enthusiastically about the formation of the Commission for Commemorating 350 Years of American Jewish History, which he chaired. Subsequently, we sought advice from Dr. Zola, as well as other commission members, particularly Dr. Michael Grunberger, then Chief of the Hebraic Section of the Library of Congress, and Dr. Michael Feldberg, then Executive Director of the American Jewish Historical Society. We are deeply grateful to all of them.

We invite you to turn the pages of the community's scrapbook.

Laura Cohen Apelbaum

Executive Director
Jewish Historical Society of Greater Washington
Lillian & Albert Small Jewish Museum

INTRODUCTION

WASHINGTON'S JEWISH STORY

Every Jewish community has a story worth telling. Each one offers its own chronology of pioneering, settlement, and institution building. Each one can enumerate its own local heroes and notable events. Each has a stirring list of "firsts," its chronicle of worthwhile accomplishments, of daughters and sons, nurtured in the community, who left a special legacy. Each claims uniqueness.

Yet, even a quick perusal of the literally hundreds of local communal histories of Jewish America indicates that communities, despite variations in region and size and density of Jewish settlement, bore a striking resemblance one to the other, with differences being those of degree rather than kind. All across America a pattern repeated itself. A small group of Jews arrived in a community, struggled to build the first tenuous institutions, usually a synagogue and a cemetery, and despite – or, perhaps, because of – their sparse numbers, managed to carve a respected place for themselves in the life of the community, engendering little hostility from their non-Jewish neighbors. Successive waves of migration, first from Central Europe and then from regions eastward, created cleavages within the totality of the Jewish people, while the religious reforms, and the traditionalists' reactions to them in the late-nineteenth century threatened the unity of *K'lal Yisrael* (the congregation of Israel). The increase in the number of Jews pushed latent anti-Jewish feelings to the surface of public awareness at this stage in the development of almost any American Jewish community.

Jews, as permanent immigrants to the United States, be it Dubuque or Detroit, Pittsburgh or Paducah, rushed to build a dazzling array of communal institutions and scampered to climb out of their relative poverty to relative wealth. Jews across America strove to prove their loyalty to their new American home, and searched for ways to balance their Jewish and their American fidelities.

Despite this almost universal pattern, communities did differ, and their institutions reflected the dynamics of the particular place. Variations in the local economy and the size of the Jewish community left an identifying stamp on each Jewish community.

Washington's Jewish community boldly bears such a stamp. While it conformed in every way to the formula of American Jewish local history and went through the same stages of growth and development that every other Jewish enclave experienced, Washington was different. Jewish Washington's uniqueness sprang from the uniqueness of the District of Columbia, itself. The national capital on the Potomac, with an economy based on commerce and service, never became home to either mass employment industries or teeming immigrant enclaves. Its physical location robbed it of the possibility of being a port city, like Baltimore, its larger neighbor to the north. Although many ambitious nineteenth-century backers and speculators hoped that the Potomac would become a major inland waterway, the city never took off as an *entrepot* for shipping and hauling.

As a result, Jews who made their way here were not the garment workers, cap makers, cigar rollers and machine operators who flocked instead to New York, Boston, Philadelphia, Baltimore, and Chicago, where factory jobs abounded. Washington's Jewish newcomers, many of whom seemed to have lived elsewhere in the United States before striking down roots in the District, had their eyes on business and commerce. Many of them may have been former factory workers yearning for the freedom and economic opportunity of self-employment. This meant that for most of its history, Washington's Jews were overwhelmingly business people, rather than laborers. The unionism and radicalism which swept through the Jewish working classes in other cities barely reared its head in the "ten miles square" of the federal city.

To conduct business one had to know English and understand American ways to a greater degree than one did to operate a sewing machine in a factory where Jewish bosses and Jewish fellow workers spoke Yiddish. Similarly, the absence of other well-organized ethnic groups created a situation in which Jews did not have to compete for jobs and political patronage with other unskilled newcomers.

Politically, residents of the District of Columbia differed from all other Americans, particularly after 1878 when, by act of Congress, they lost the right to elect their own local officials, make their own laws, or vote for president or representatives to Congress. For Jews, seeking to create a community within a community, this particular political configuration would be significant. Washington, through the 1960s, lacked the municipal politics of a "normal" city. No local office holders or political bosses appealed to voters from diverse ethnic groups, currying favor with them, passing out patronage, balancing tickets, and hoping for their votes in return. Not only did Washington's Jews not develop a local Jewish political infrastructure, such as sprang up in New York, Chicago, and Baltimore, but, if they sought help, they had to turn to Congress. If they had local needs, they had to seek national assistance.

This blurring of the local and the national in Washington constitutes the most striking characteristic of public life, Jewish and non-Jewish, in the capital city. Local issues demanded national solutions. Local problems were addressed by a national body. Jewish Washington, from the late-nineteenth century on, has played a role in national Jewish affairs far beyond what its numbers would have warranted. Jewish Washington took on tasks for American Jews as a whole.

From the 1860s on, Washington's Jews as individuals, and through their self-appointed leaders—like Simon Wolf and Adolphus Solomons—expressed their solidarity and sympathy with their sisters and brothers enduring oppression elsewhere. While Jews around the United States joined in various ways in the chorus of protests over anti-semitism abroad, the direct negotiations with presidents and secretaries of states fell to the Washington power brokers, who in essence became American Jewry's ambassadors-at-large.

In the twentieth century Jews flocked to Washington not just for small business, but for work in the federal government. With the advent of the New Deal, Jews like Supreme Court Justice Felix Frankfurter and labor-leader Sidney Hillman, to name but two, played a prominent role in national affairs. Jewish social scientists, social workers, lawyers, accountants, and bureaucrats were becoming as common in Washington as Jewish grocers and haberdashers had been a generation earlier.

Equally important, by the third and fourth decades of the twentieth century, the eyes of Jewish America were taking on more and more of a national and international focus. Since the days of Simon Wolf, Jews had pleaded with the United States government to provide assistance to their Jewish sisters and brothers in distress abroad. The dynamics of the post-World War I world seemed to call for more systematic and intense efforts in dealing with the government and in mobilizing the Jewish community. The ravages of the war on the Jewish communities of Europe had given rise to the Joint Distribution Committee, a decidedly non-Zionist body, while the flowering of Zionist sentiment in America and the burgeoning Jewish settlements in Palestine propelled American Jews into founding the United Palestine Appeal. The ascendancy to power of Hitler in 1933 and the barring of Jewish emigration to Palestine brought the developing international perspective into even sharper focus.

Washington thus took on even greater significance in American Jewish affairs. In 1938 the B'nai B'rith moved its national offices to Washington, D.C., and over the course of the next decades the American Jewish Committee, the American Jewish Congress, the National Council of Jewish Women, and the Jewish Labor Committee set up national offices in the capital. A cadre of national Jewish agency officials now worked and lived in the capital.

As the community grew, organizational life became more centralized. In 1933, the various synagogue charities and other social-service groups united to form the Jewish Social Service Agency. In 1937 the United Jewish Appeal initiated coordination of all local fundraising for overseas and some local purposes. The Jewish Community Council was founded in 1938 as a form of democratically elected, voluntary Jewish "government" empowered to address issues of concern to the entire Jewish community and to coordinate Jews' relations with non-Jewish Washington.

During and after World War II Washington's Jewish population continued to grow rapidly. Even as Jewish institutional life in Washington flowered in the 1950s, Jews joined the general migration out of the city and into the suburbs. This relocation transformed Washington from the hub of Jewish life to the periphery, as Jewish institutions and the bulk of the area's rapidly growing Jewish population shifted to Montgomery County and Northern Virginia.

Numerous synagogues decided to follow the population into the suburban areas. Significantly, in 1969 the Jewish Community Center sold its Sixteenth Street building and relocated, along with the Jewish Social Service Agency and the Hebrew Home for the Aged, to a large complex in Rockville, Maryland. By 1977, a Jewish Community Center had been established in Fairfax, Virginia, as well.

Despite the fact that Jewish institutional life had moved beyond the beltway, events of importance to Jews still took place within the District. Jews worldwide agitated on behalf of Soviet Jewry, but only in Washington could a daily vigil at noon, started in 1970, be mounted by the Jewish Community Council in front of the Soviet Embassy. Indeed, the community council and other organizations continued to play a national role in Jewish affairs.

Even as the locus of local Jewish life shifted to the suburbs, a significant number of Jews still remained strongly committed to the city. Some institutions, including many synagogues, affirmatively chose not to leave Washington.

A dramatic sign of a resurgent and assertive Jewish community in the city was the founding of a new District of Columbia Jewish Community Center in 1979. In 1988 the center began negotiations with District officials to buy back the Sixteenth Street building, which had been sold to the city in 1969, in order to transform it once again into a hub of Jewish life in Washington. Center officials signed the sales contract in the summer of 1990 and after a major restoration, the Washington DCJCC opened in 1997. Other Jewish institutions have followed in moving back to the city.

The renaissance of Jewish cultural life in the city in the 1970s and 1980s paralleled a literal rebirth of political life with the advent of home rule. As Washingtonians plunged into electoral politics for the first time in a century, individual Jews and Jewish organizations quickly became a part of the political scene. As political life returned to the city, Jews extended their longtime involvement with federal issues to the local government.

From the start, Jews built a highly self-conscious community, aware of their special visibility in the capital.

Hasia Diner, Ph.D.

Paul S. and Sylvia Steinberg Professor of American Jewish History
The Skirball Department of Hebrew and Judaic Studies
New York University

Adapted from Hasia Diner, Fifty Years of Jewish Self-Governance: The Jewish Community Council of Greater Washington, 1989 and from Hasia R. Diner and Steven J. Diner, "Washington's Jewish Community: Separate But Not Apart" in Urban Odyssey: A Multicultural History of Washington, D.C., 1996.

FIRST ENTRIES

Only a few Jews had found their way to the nation's capital prior to the 1850s. Fleeing harsh restrictions, German-speaking Jewish immigrants began arriving in the decade before the Civil War.

By 1880, Washington's Jewish immigrant community of 1,500 sustained two synagogues and a variety of social organizations. The community took responsibility for fellow Jews and pressed Congress and the President on national and international issues.

1869: This view looking east from 17th Street, N.W., shows 19th-century Washington, D.C., from the White House to the Capitol.

FIRST JEWS, FIRST CONGREGATION

In 1843, there were too few Jews to form a ten-man *minyan*. Less than a decade later, the capital's first Jewish congregation was formed.

"The Rev. S. Weil recite(d) the prayer for the Government in both Hebrew and English. The Haphtorah is read in German ... The Congregation is prospering greatly, numbering about ninety members."

The Jewish Messenger,
December 11, 1863

1828: New arrival Captain Alfred Mordecai was assigned to the Washington Arsenal. When his infant son Frank died in 1843, the city lacked a *minyan* of ten Jewish men to say the memorial prayer, *Kaddish*, at the funeral. Mordecai resigned his position in 1861 and left Washington rather than serve against his native North Carolina in the Civil War.

Washington's first known Jewish resident, Isaac Polock, arrived from Savannah in 1795. An early land speculator in the new capital city, he built stately homes. In 1828, Captain Alfred Mordecai was assigned to the Washington Arsenal. His daughter, Rosa, born in 1839, was the first Jewish child born in Washington.

Dwindling economic prospects and failed revolutionary movements in Central Europe precipitated a wave of immigration in the 1840s and 1850s. Some immigrants who arrived in port cities like New York and Baltimore later moved to Washington. Brothers Amnon and Bendiza Behrend immigrated to New York from the German city of Rodenberg in 1849. By the 1850s, each brother had opened a business along Seventh Street, N.W. The new arrivals became part of the small but thriving German immigrant community in Washington.

In 1852, 21 men met in a Pennsylvania Avenue home to form Washington's first Jewish congregation. Each contributed one dollar in dues.

Late 1700s: Washington's first Jewish resident, Isaac Polock, built these brick mansions at 21st Street and Pennsylvania Avenue, west of the White House. Known as the Six Buildings, they initially housed the U.S. State Department and Secretary of the Navy. Later they were home to Secretaries of State James Madison and William Seward, and to General Sam Houston.

1845: This "Reise-Pass" exemplifies the restrictions faced by Jews in German states. While Bernhard Behrend was traveling from his native Rodenberg to Frankfurt, he was required to carry this pass. Behrend's physical characteristics are listed on the left—including his age, height, and hair color.

Early 1850s: Hungarian freedom fighter Emanuel Lulley immigrated to New York and, by 1853, had moved to Washington with his wife Cecilia and their children. Their granddaughter Bertha married Jonas Hechinger. The Hechinger's first child, Sidney, later founded the Washington chain of hardware stores.

Washington Hebrew—the first Jewish congregation in the nation's capital—is the only one in the country with a Congressional charter. The congregation petitioned Congress (constitutionally responsible for local law) for legislation ensuring its right to own property in Washington. President Franklin Pierce signed "An Act for the Benefit of the Hebrew Congregation in the city of Washington" on June 2, 1856.

WASHINGTON'S FIRST CONGREGATION

1863: The congregation purchased this former Methodist Episcopal Church on 8th Street, N.W.

1856: Washington Hebrew's Congressional Charter

1860s: Hannah Mundheim (above) headed Washington Hebrew's visiting nursing corps. Her husband, Simon (right), was the *shochet* (ritual butcher) for Washington Hebrew. Their daughter, Sarah, married Leopold Karpeles.

A HOUSE DIVIDED

During the Civil war, the women of the Washington Hebrew Congregation raised money for the U.S. Sanitary Commission, which administered wartime relief to soldiers and their families. The congregation's visiting nursing corps ministered to injured Jewish soldiers. Unclaimed bodies of Jewish war dead were buried in the congregation's cemetery. When President Abraham Lincoln was shot, a Jewish physician—Charles Liebermann—was among the doctors called to his bedside.

Some Jewish soldiers who had come to Washington during the war stayed in the capital.

April 1865: The Union Army marches down Pennsylvania Avenue in victory (background image.)

1865 and beyond: Among the Jewish soldiers who lived in Washington after the Civil War were Abraham Hart (above), Adajah Behrend (above left), and Bernard Nordlinger (left). Hart, a veteran of the Union Army, practiced law. Behrend, who served as a Union Army hospital steward, became a doctor after receiving a medical degree from Georgetown University in 1866. Nordlinger, a former Confederate war prisoner, opened a shoe store on M Street in Georgetown.

LEOPOLD **K**ARPELES

"My dedication to my country's flag rests on my ardent belief in the noblest of causes, equality for all."
—Leopold Karpeles, 1870

April 19, 1865: Among those marching in President Lincoln's funeral procession (background image), were 125 men of Washington Hebrew Congregation. The Lansburgh brothers donated $500 toward the first monument to the President's memory. It still stands in front of the old City Hall at 4th and D Streets, N.W.

M. A. DILLON, Commander in Chief.

MEDAL OF HONOR LEGION.

ELIGIBILITY:
Personal Identity, Legal Possession of the Medal, and Good Character.

1860s: Leopold Karpeles carried the regimental colors for the Union Army in more than 15 battles, including Gettysburg. He was awarded the Congressional Medal of Honor for rallying the troops during the Battle of the Wilderness in Virginia. Later wounded, Karpeles was brought to Washington, where he recuperated under the care of Washington Hebrew's visiting nurses.

After the war, he married one of his nurses, Sarah Mundheim, and became a clerk in the U.S. Postal Department. On the stationery of the newly formed Medal of Honor Legion, Karpeles wrote this letter concerning his military pension.

During the Civil War years, business boomed, and Jewish communal life took root in the nation's capital.

GROWTH AND PROSPERITY

During the Civil War, the Jewish population grew from 200 to nearly 2,000. Most newcomers were Jewish merchants arriving to serve the wartime boom. The demand for food, lodging, and household goods sent prices skyrocketing—enriching tailors, boarding house operators, and business proprietors. Of the more than 450 restaurants and bars that opened during the Civil War, six were kosher restaurants.

Social life thrived as well. Harmonie Circle and Select Assembly hosted masked balls for the Jewish holiday of Purim and other soirees to provide fellowship for Jewish merchants. The Washington Literary and Dramatic Association met on Sunday afternoons. The first Washington lodge of B'nai B'rith was started in 1864, and 25 Jews joined local Masonic lodges between 1853 and 1865.

1890: Young Jewish men and women enjoy a summer gathering. Isaac Nordlinger, son of Civil War veteran Bernard Nordlinger, is wearing a bow tie in the front row. Minnie Lansburgh, daughter of department store owner Gustav Lansburgh, stands in the second row on the far left.

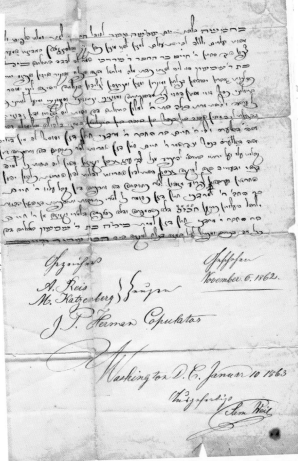

1862: The marriage between Henry Baum and Bettie Dreifus, as agreed to in this *ketubah* (marriage contract), took place in Washington, D.C. Civil War travel restrictions prevented the groom from traveling to his bride's home in Alexandria, Virginia.

1860s: Brothers Gustav and Max Lansburgh opened Baltimore House (above), a small fancy goods store on C Street and the predecessor to the landmark Lansburgh's Department Store on 7th Street, N.W.

1864: Ads for a variety of Jewish businesses from the city directory.

LOCAL AND NATIONAL LEADER

A ADOLPHUS SOLOMONS (1826-1910)

Adolphus Solomons counseled local and national Jewish leaders on important issues of the day. An observant Sephardic Jew, he prayed at home, where he kept a *Ner Tamid* (eternal light) brought with him from New York's Shearith Israel, the nation's first congregation. Solomons' bookstore supplied stationery to the House of Representatives during the Civil War.

As the Civil War got underway, Solomons played a pivotal role in convincing President Lincoln to allow Jews to become military chaplains. He served in the Washington, D.C. House of Delegates (1871) and on the Presidential Inauguration Committee for Ulysses S. Grant (1873). In 1876 he raised funds from New York financier Jacob Schiff for a synagogue building for a new congregation, Adas Israel. In 1881, he helped Clara Barton found the American Red Cross.

Solomons later returned to New York to administer the Baron de Hirsch Fund, an agency providing Jewish immigrants with vocational training and assistance.

Early 1870s: Solomons declined President Grant's request to serve as governor of Washington, D.C. (during a brief period of self-government), because the position required work on Saturday, the Jewish Sabbath.

Inset: Solomons as a young man.

Late 1800s: Solomons entertained many guests—including Charles Dickens—in his elegant home at 1205 K Street, N.W. (background image). Here and in his bookshop, he advised fellow Jews on causes such as the need for Jewish chaplains in the military.

"We passed a pleasant Sabbath with Mr. Adolphus Solomons whose place of business (on) Pennsylvania Avenue is the resort of men of letters....
We were pleased to find Mr. S doing so well in the capital, especially as he is one of the very few Israelites there who observe the Sabbath."
— The Jewish Messenger, January 24, 1862

1903: Sketch of Adas Israel synagogue in *The Washington Post.*

A SECOND CONGREGATION

In its early years, Washington Hebrew was an exemplar of Jewish tradition. Change began, however, with liturgy—eliminating certain prayers and using German or English instead of Hebrew in others. Eventually the congregation authorized a choir and included an organ in the service.

In 1869, a group of about 30 members resigned over these changes and founded Adas Israel Congregation. Washington Hebrew called itself Reform; Adas Israel was strictly orthodox. In 1876—just in time for the nation's Centennial celebration—Adas Israel built a new synagogue at the corner of 6th and G Streets, N.W. President Ulysses S. Grant attended the three-hour dedication service.

1869: After resigning from Washington Hebrew Congregation, Bendiza Behrend became the first president of the new Adas Israel Congregation.

June 9, 1876: The presence of President Ulysses S. Grant at the dedication of the new Adas Israel synagogue—and his $10 donation—held special meaning. As a Union Army general, Grant had issued Order No. 11 expelling Jews "as a class" from Tennessee, southern Illinois, and Kentucky. President Lincoln revoked the order. Although Grant never apologized, he privately referred to his action as "that obnoxious order."

Circa 1900: Adas Israel synagogue at its 6th and G Streets location.

As Washington Hebrew gradually drifted from strict tradition, a new orthodox congregation formed and built its own synagogue.

For his 70th birthday, Wolf's daughter, Florence Gotthold, compiled three books with more than 400 personal messages from leaders of the time—including Supreme Court Justice Oliver Wendell Holmes, Mark Twain, and Presidents Grover Cleveland, Theodore Roosevelt, and William Howard Taft.

FRIEND OF PRESIDENTS

SIMON WOLF (1836-1923)

One of the most influential Jewish leaders of the late 19th and early 20th centuries, Simon Wolf studied law in Cleveland before moving to Washington in 1862. He was an eloquent orator and advocate on behalf of Jewish issues. In 1869, when Russia exiled 30,000 Jewish families from its border areas, Wolf appealed to President Grant to intercede. In 1903, when Jews fell victim to the Kishineff *pogrom*, he helped collect 13,000 signatures protesting the Russian government's actions.

Wolf served as president of Washington Hebrew Congregation in 1872, and as both local and national president of B'nai B'rith. A columnist for *The Jewish Messenger,* Wolf often commented on Jewish life in the capital city.

"If there were more Simon Wolfs in this world, humanity would be the gainer."

— Christian Heurich, Washington brewer and philanthropist, 1906

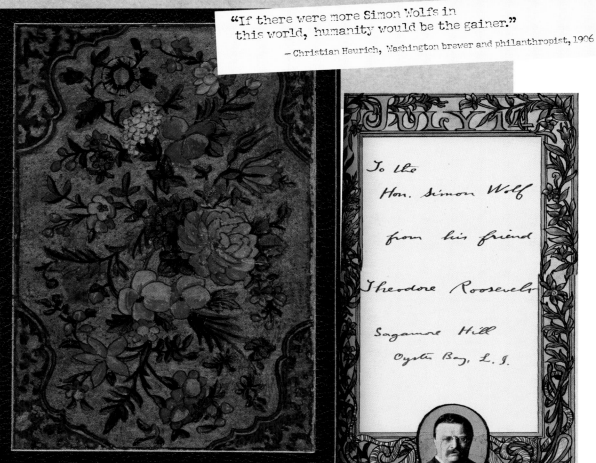

THE PRESIDENTS I HAVE KNOWN FROM 1860 TO 1918

SIMON WOLF

1918: Wolf's 1918 autobiography, *Presidents I Have Known,* was aptly named. When President Grant named him Recorder of Deeds for Washington in 1869, Wolf became one of the first Jews in the city to hold public office. In 1881, President James Garfield appointed him Consul General to Egypt.

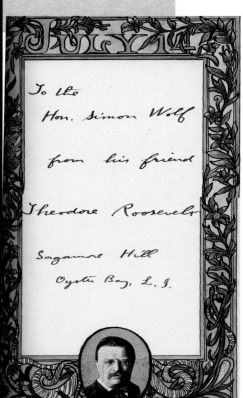

To the Hon. Simon Wolf from his friend Theodore Roosevelt

Sagamore Hill Oyster Bay, L.I.

1880s-1920s

Early 1900s: Cantor William and Jennie Tash, shown here in their wedding photo, arrived from Russia around 1911 and settled on 5th Street, N.W. Until Tash found work, the family took in boarders, and the children sold papers on street corners.

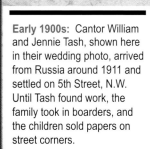

THE SCRAPBOOK THICKENS

By 1880, many of Washington's 1,500 Jews were second-generation Americans and established merchants. Most practiced Reform Judaism. They were soon joined by a new wave of Jewish immigrants fleeing Eastern Europe's *pogroms*, poverty, and forced military service. Mostly Orthodox Jews, the newcomers settled in downtown neighborhoods and formed small *shuls* within walking distance of their homes.

By 1920, Washington's Jewish population numbered 10,000. Some Jews established local chapters of Zionist organizations and sent hard-earned dollars to support Jewish settlement in Palestine.

CABINET PORTRAIT

NEIGHBORHOODS

Washington's Jews were dispersed throughout the city.

Unlike other Eastern cities, where Jews lived in concentrated immigrant neighborhoods, Washington's Jews lived and worked throughout the city. Jewish enclaves sprang up along major thoroughfares lined with small businesses and rowhouses.

By the early 1910s, the more settled German-American Jews had begun moving north and west away from their downtown businesses, toward Cleveland Park and Forest Hills. More recent Yiddish-speaking immigrants lived "above the shop" in downtown neighborhoods. They later moved north to settle in neighborhoods east of Rock Creek Park such as Petworth, Brightwood, and Crestwood.

Georgetown: Meyer and Lillie Levy moved to Georgetown from Southwest Washington around 1915. In the early 1930s, their son Sam opened a men's clothing store. Shown above is his store at 3059 M Street in 1940. A leading merchant and real estate investor in the neighborhood, Sam Levy became known as "the mayor of Georgetown."

4¹/₂ Street, Southwest: Harry Wender (right) lived above his parents' grocery store at 1305 4¹/₂ Street. He later led efforts to modernize and pave 4¹/₂ Street, and served as president of the D.C. Federation of Citizens Associations and chairman of the D.C. Recreation Board.

4¹/₂ Street, Southwest: Jewish-owned businesses lined the cobblestone streets near 4¹/₂ Street, S.W. Harry Chidakel's barbershop (above) was on 7th Street, and Aaron Berkman's grocery (left) was at 3rd and G. Isaac and Cyril Levy, (right) with their 12 children, opened Levy's Busy Corner department store on 4¹/₂ Street in 1888.

Petworth:
For many, the Petworth neighborhood offered the prospect of owning their first home. In the 1920s, Morris Cafritz and other developers built thousands of rowhouses like those shown here in the 4500 block of 13th Street, N.W. Jewish life centered around the neighborhood synagogue, Har Zion, on Georgia Avenue.

Cleveland Park:
When Tina and Fred Gichner moved their family from 4½ Street, S.W., to Cleveland Park in 1909, they were among the first Jewish families in that neighborhood. They are pictured here with their children outside their home at 3220 Highland Place, N.W.

Front row, left to right: Bill, Tina, Fred, Joe, and Hanna Gichner.
Back row, left to right: Jacob, Henry.

H Street, Northeast: Many Russian Jewish immigrants settled along H Street, N.E., in the early 1900s. Jacob and Esther Love owned a shoe repair shop at 1407 H Street (above). Daniel Gilbert ran a bike shop at 1370 H Street (left). Ezras Israel synagogue at 8th and I Streets (below) anchored the tight-knit neighborhood.

18th and Columbia Road:
Many Jewish families lived on Lanier Place and the surrounding streets near 18th and Columbia Road, N.W., in the 1920s. *Chazan* Moshe Yoelson moved to the neighborhood from 4½ Street, S.W., when his son—entertainer Al Jolson—bought him a house at 1787 Lanier Place. Shown here are Jeanette Naiman (Danziger) and her niece Irma Naiman (Greenspoon), who lived next door to each other at 1747 and 1749 Lanier Place.

1890s-1920s: Jewish-owned shops populated the 7th Street neighborhood, including King's Palace and Goldenberg's, "The Dependable Store." Saks & Company sold "everything that men and boys wear."

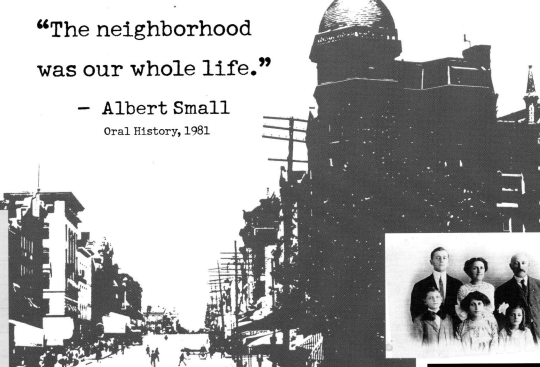

> "The neighborhood was our whole life."
>
> — Albert Small
> Oral History, 1981

Anchored by the bustling Center Market on Pennsylvania Avenue, 7th Street, N.W., became the city's main business district and a center of Jewish residential and religious life.

1899: Isadore Small (back row, right) is shown here with his family, including son Albert (front row, left). He lived at 725 5th Street, N.W., just a few short blocks from his 7th Street hardware store.

SEVENTH STREET, NORTHWEST

> "We got to Baltimore on a Saturday morning in 1911 and came right to Washington. On Sunday, my uncle took me… [to] 7th Street, and he got me a new suit and made me an American."
>
> — Israel Orlove
> Oral History, 1981

Many German-speaking Jewish immigrants got their start on 7th Street, N.W. Isadore Small owned a hardware store on the site of what is now the Verizon Center. Amid smaller furniture, jewelry, and millinery shops, Hahn's opened its flagship shoe store at 7th and K in 1898. Several Jewish merchants with shops along 7th Street expanded them into fashionable department stores.

By the 1890s, Russian immigrants began moving to the area and opening small businesses. Barnett Cohen and son-in-law Hymen Goldman supplied local merchants with wholesale jewelry, hosiery, and gloves. Mayer Dodek opened Dodek's Furniture & Clothing on 7th Street between H and I Streets in 1898.

1898: Mayer Dodek, a 7th Street merchant, left his business to fight in the Spanish-American War. His son Samuel's first job was running errands for Kahn Optical Company on 7th Street. Samuel Dodek later became one of Washington's leading obstetricians.

FLAGSHIPS ON SEVENTH STREET

1893: Solomon Kann and his three sons opened S. Kann & Co. Their motto "the customer is right" clashed with their "strictly cash" policy. Even the request of the President's wife, Mrs. Grover Cleveland, to charge a purchase was politely refused.

1882: The former Baltimore House expanded to a grand 24,000-square-foot department store renamed Lansburgh & Brothers. A downtown landmark for 114 years, it featured the first commercial elevator in Washington and a skylight that enabled shoppers to see the color of imported fabrics and fine silks in natural light.

1896: Alexander and Moses Hecht launched Hecht's Greater Stores. In 1924, they opened this new store—the first to promote nationally advertised brands—at 7th and F Streets. Hecht's was the longest surviving link to the early glory days of the downtown department stores.

1913: This photo shows Barnett Cohen (left) and Hymen Goldman (center) in front of their wholesale goods store at 622 Pennsylvania Avenue, N.W

1899: A downtown fixture that first opened in 1869, Rich's Shoe Store is shown here at its 10th and F Street location.

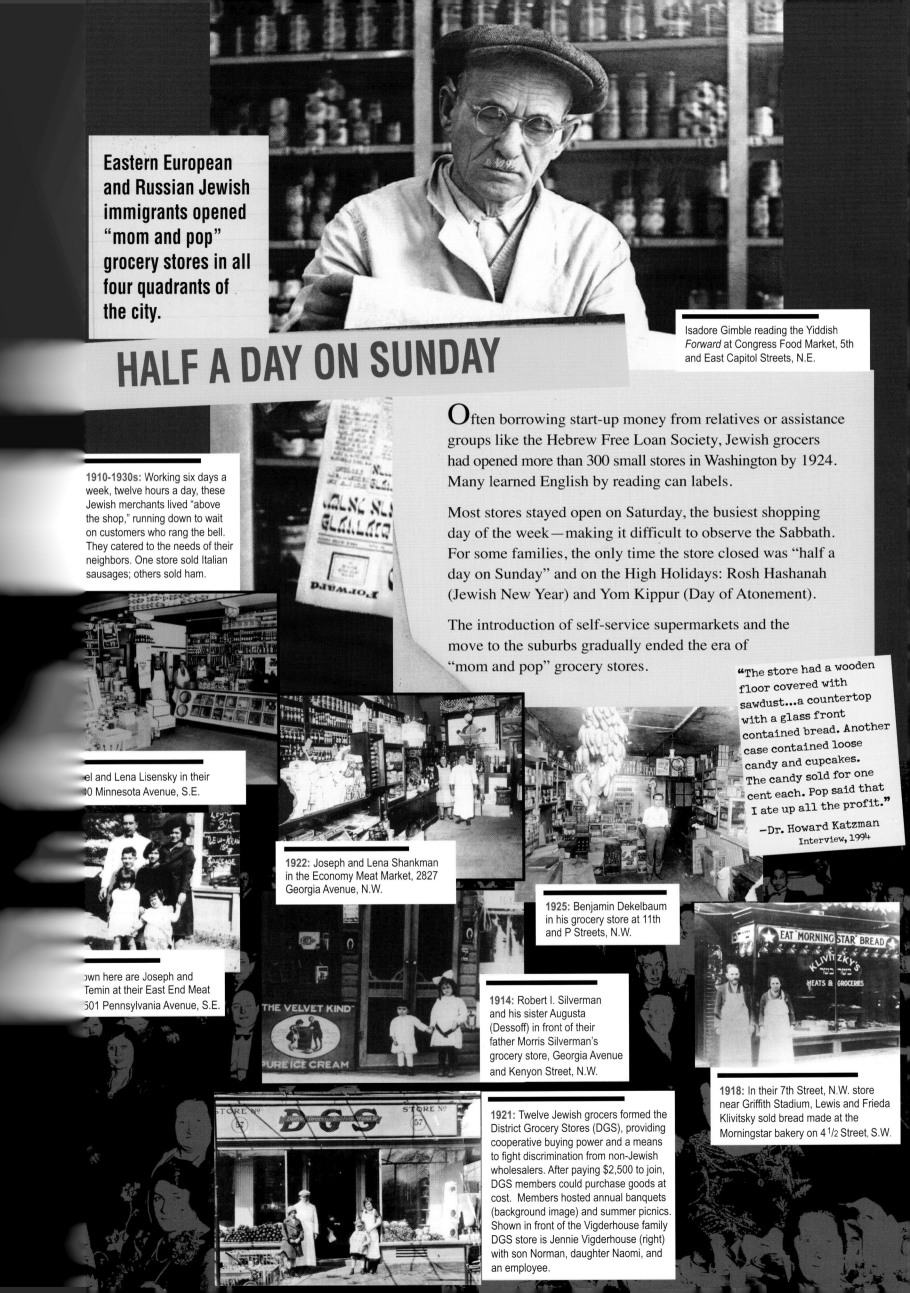

Eastern European and Russian Jewish immigrants opened "mom and pop" grocery stores in all four quadrants of the city.

Isadore Gimble reading the Yiddish *Forward* at Congress Food Market, 5th and East Capitol Streets, N.E.

HALF A DAY ON SUNDAY

1910-1930s: Working six days a week, twelve hours a day, these Jewish merchants lived "above the shop," running down to wait on customers who rang the bell. They catered to the needs of their neighbors. One store sold Italian sausages; others sold ham.

Often borrowing start-up money from relatives or assistance groups like the Hebrew Free Loan Society, Jewish grocers had opened more than 300 small stores in Washington by 1924. Many learned English by reading can labels.

Most stores stayed open on Saturday, the busiest shopping day of the week—making it difficult to observe the Sabbath. For some families, the only time the store closed was "half a day on Sunday" and on the High Holidays: Rosh Hashanah (Jewish New Year) and Yom Kippur (Day of Atonement).

The introduction of self-service supermarkets and the move to the suburbs gradually ended the era of "mom and pop" grocery stores.

"The store had a wooden floor covered with sawdust...a countertop with a glass front contained bread. Another case contained loose candy and cupcakes. The candy sold for one cent each. Pop said that I ate up all the profit."
—Dr. Howard Katzman
Interview, 1994

...el and Lena Lisensky in their ...0 Minnesota Avenue, S.E.

1922: Joseph and Lena Shankman in the Economy Meat Market, 2827 Georgia Avenue, N.W.

1925: Benjamin Dekelbaum in his grocery store at 11th and P Streets, N.W.

...own here are Joseph and ...Temin at their East End Meat ...501 Pennsylvania Avenue, S.E.

1914: Robert I. Silverman and his sister Augusta (Dessoff) in front of their father Morris Silverman's grocery store, Georgia Avenue and Kenyon Street, N.W.

1918: In their 7th Street, N.W. store near Griffith Stadium, Lewis and Frieda Klivitsky sold bread made at the Morningstar bakery on 4 1/2 Street, S.W.

1921: Twelve Jewish grocers formed the District Grocery Stores (DGS), providing cooperative buying power and a means to fight discrimination from non-Jewish wholesalers. After paying $2,500 to join, DGS members could purchase goods at cost. Members hosted annual banquets (background image) and summer picnics. Shown in front of the Vigderhouse family DGS store is Jennie Vigderhouse (right) with son Norman, daughter Naomi, and an employee.

ON WITH THE SHOW

In 1907, A.C. Mayer joined Aaron and Julian Brylawski to open Washington's first Jewish-owned movie house, the Palace Theater, at 307 9th Street, N.W. For a nickel, patrons watched melodramas, comedies, and live vaudeville skits. The exterior was studded with 1,684 electric lights. The lit façade was said to be one of the prettiest sights in the city at night. The Brylawskis later formed the Cosmos Theater Company and assembled a chain of movie houses.

1924: Fred Kogod and Max Burka bought the Princess Theater on H Street, N.E., and launched the K-B Amusement Company. Their chain brought first-run features to the Washington area for more than 60 years. The K-B owned Apex Theater, shown here, opened at 4813 Massachusetts Avenue, N.W., in 1940. Like other public accommodations in Washington, movie theaters remained segregated through the early 1950s. K-B was among the Washington exhibitors to integrate their theaters in 1953.

1910: Other Jewish-owned theaters opened in the city. The Leader, shown here at 507 9th Street, N.W., was one of several owned by Sidney Lust.

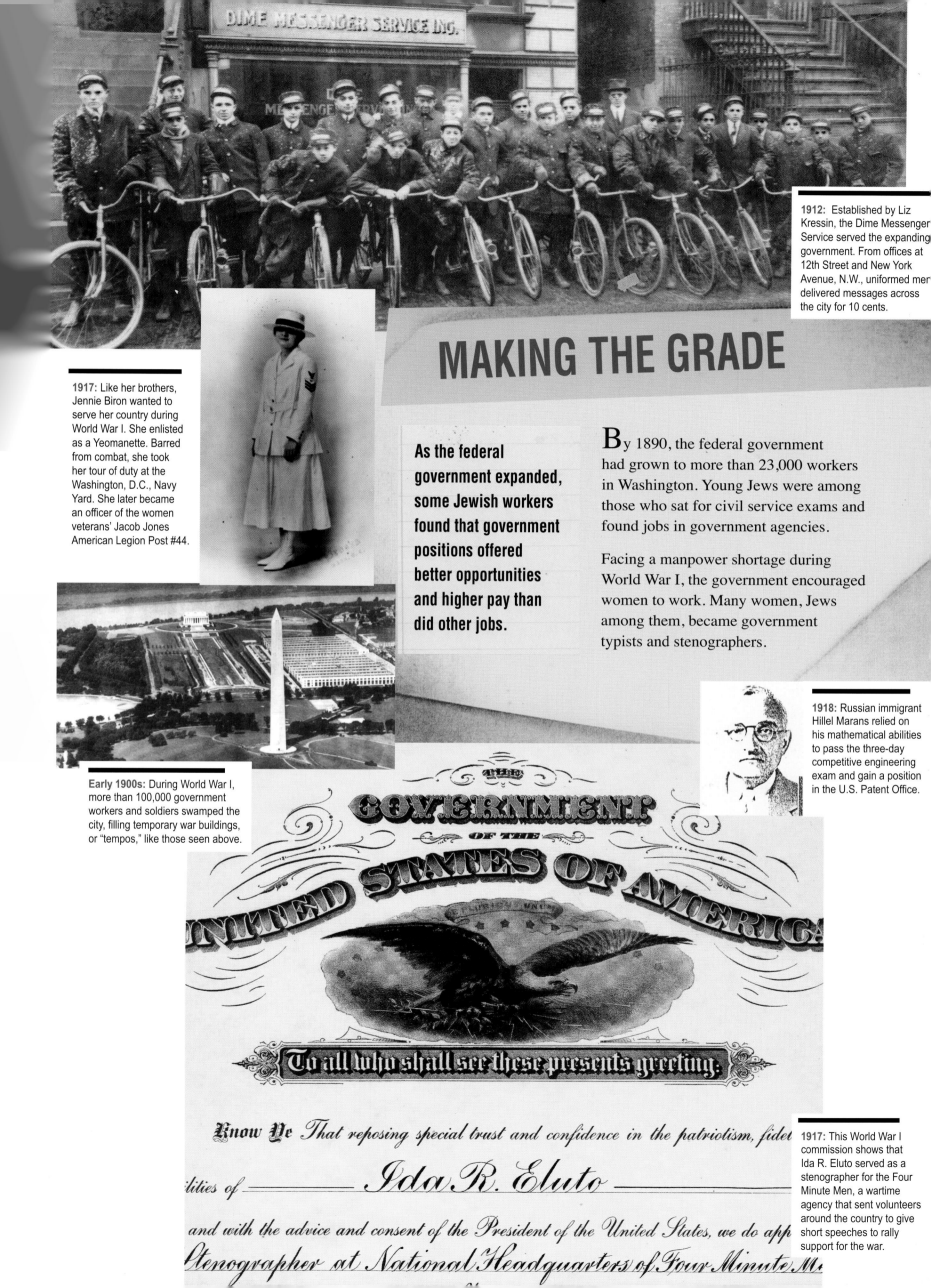

1912: Established by Liz Kressin, the Dime Messenger Service served the expanding government. From offices at 12th Street and New York Avenue, N.W., uniformed men delivered messages across the city for 10 cents.

MAKING THE GRADE

1917: Like her brothers, Jennie Biron wanted to serve her country during World War I. She enlisted as a Yeomanette. Barred from combat, she took her tour of duty at the Washington, D.C., Navy Yard. She later became an officer of the women veterans' Jacob Jones American Legion Post #44.

As the federal government expanded, some Jewish workers found that government positions offered better opportunities and higher pay than did other jobs.

By 1890, the federal government had grown to more than 23,000 workers in Washington. Young Jews were among those who sat for civil service exams and found jobs in government agencies.

Facing a manpower shortage during World War I, the government encouraged women to work. Many women, Jews among them, became government typists and stenographers.

Early 1900s: During World War I, more than 100,000 government workers and soldiers swamped the city, filling temporary war buildings, or "tempos," like those seen above.

1918: Russian immigrant Hillel Marans relied on his mathematical abilities to pass the three-day competitive engineering exam and gain a position in the U.S. Patent Office.

THE GOVERNMENT OF THE UNITED STATES OF AMERICA

To all who shall see these presents greeting:

Know Ye That reposing special trust and confidence in the patriotism, fidel...

...ilities of ———— Ida R. Eluto ————

and with the advice and consent of the President of the United States, we do app...

Stenographer at National Headquarters of Four Minute M...

1917: This World War I commission shows that Ida R. Eluto served as a stenographer for the Four Minute Men, a wartime agency that sent volunteers around the country to give short speeches to rally support for the war.

A triad of synagogues dominated the 7th Street neighborhood, while other congregations formed throughout the city.

SYNAGOGUE GROWTH

The city's three oldest congregations—Washington Hebrew, Adas Israel, and Ohev Sholom—were located within three city blocks of each other. They represented the spectrum of Jewish religious practice at the time: Reform, Conservative, and Orthodox. On High Holidays, police closed I Street to traffic to permit worshippers to walk between the *shuls*. On Sabbath mornings, young people from the synagogues socialized at a small triangular park at 5th and I Streets, N.W. Women created a voice in the traditionally male-dominated synagogues by founding religious schools and sisterhoods.

Between 1880 and the 1920s, several new synagogues—mostly Orthodox—opened throughout the city.

1908: Adas Israel completed a new, larger building at 6th and I Streets, N.W. Designed by Baltimore architect Louis Levi, the sanctuary sat 1,600 and featured the Moorish architecture popular at the time. Originally Orthodox, the congregation affiliated with the Conservative movement in 1928.

1905: Carrie Simon, wife of Rabbi Abram Simon, founded Washington Hebrew's ladies auxiliary. In 1913, she brought together representatives from sisterhoods across the nation to create Reform Judaism's National Federation of Temple Sisterhoods.

1906: Nearly twenty years after holding their first services above Myer Fisher's 7th Street clothing store, Ohev Sholom Congregation purchased a church at 5th and I Streets, N.W. They replaced the steeple with a dome and converted it to a synagogue. The Orthodox congregation was the first formed by the city's Russian Jews.

1898: Washington Hebrew built an impressive new structure on the site of its original synagogue near 8th and I Streets, N.W. President William McKinley attended the cornerstone laying ceremony.

1859: Beth El Hebrew Congregation, Northern Virginia's oldest, was established. The German-speaking members built their first synagogue, seen here, in 1871 on Washington Street in Alexandria.

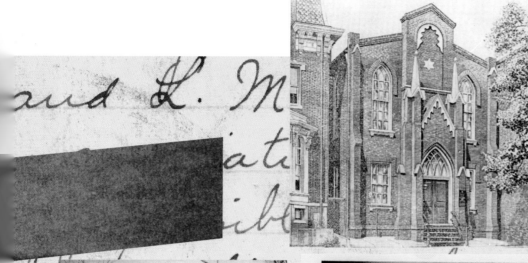

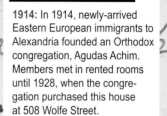

1914: In 1914, newly-arrived Eastern European immigrants to Alexandria founded an Orthodox congregation, Agudas Achim. Members met in rented rooms until 1928, when the congregation purchased this house at 508 Wolfe Street.

1914: Tifereth Israel began meeting in private homes near 14th and U Streets, N.W. By the early 1920s, the congregation moved to a converted house at 14th and Euclid. The congregation's choir is shown here in 1928.

1887: *Chazan* Moshe Yoelson, father of famed entertainer Al Jolson, served the Talmud Torah congregation at 467 E Street, S.W., from 1892 through the 1920s. Formed in 1887, the Orthodox congregation met in Isaac Levy's department store on 4½ Street, S.W., before they completed this synagogue in 1906.

1915: Georgetown's Orthodox Jewish community acquired a private home at 2801 N Street, N.W., for the new Kesher Israel Congregation. This new Orthodox synagogue was built on the same site in 1931.

> **"The big task with us women is that of encouraging one another to take the reins in our hands and stimulate our women to the task of religious self-assertion."**
>
> **— Carrie Simon**
> Address to National Federation of Temple Sisterhoods Convention, 1921

1920: Har-Zion Congregation formed on Georgia Avenue in the Petworth neighborhood. In 1936, the Orthodox congregation merged with Voliner Anshe Sfard, a small immigrant *shul* on 4½ Street, S.W. The combined congregation took the name Beth Sholom and built a new synagogue, shown above, at 8th and Shepherd Streets, N.W., two years later.

1925: B'nai Israel Congregation and Talmud Torah began meeting in a house at 4708 Georgia Avenue. In 1929, the congregation converted a former church at 14th and Emerson Streets, N.W., to synagogue use.

1897: Minutes of the first Adas Israel Sisterhood meeting (background image).

1914: The first anniversary dance of the Young Women's Hebrew Association takes place.

THE CENTER OF IT ALL

Washington's new Jewish Community Center provided activities for youth, adults, and the elderly.

In 1911, a group of Jewish men in their early twenties formed the Young Men's Hebrew Association (YMHA). The Young Women's Hebrew Association (YWHA) followed in 1913. The organizations hosted musicales, dances, picnics, and athletic events for the hundreds of Jewish youth in the city. Together, the YMHA and YWHA also served the thousands of Jewish servicemen posted in Washington during World War I.

After the war, the need for a larger community center in the capital city was evident. A five-year campaign led to the opening of the Jewish Community Center (JCC) at 16th and Q Streets, N.W., in 1926. The JCC also served as the meeting place for many Jewish organizations.

1918: The Young Men's Hebrew Association (YMHA) moved to this building at 11th and Pennsylvania Avenue, N.W. During World War I, the YMHA expanded its programs to accommodate Jewish servicemen in the American and Allied armed forces.

1920s: Berte and Sylvia Luber enjoy the view from the roof of the new JCC.

1925: President Calvin Coolidge spoke during the cornerstone-laying ceremony of the 16th and Q Street building on May 3, 1925. The national Jewish Welfare Board provided an initial $50,000 for the Center. Developer Morris Cafritz and local Jewish leader Joseph Wilner led the $500,000 building campaign.

"This edifice...is a fine example for other communities. It speaks a purpose to uphold an ancient and noble philosophy and to assure that such philosophy shall always be adapted to the requirements of changing times."

— President Calvin Coolidge, May 3, 1925

Laying of Corner Stone
JEWISH COMMUNITY CENTER

"The National Center"

PUBLISHED BY THE
JEWISH COMMUNITY CENTER
WASHINGTON, D.
OCTOBER 15, 1924

ADOPTED DESIGN FOR THE NEW JEWISH COMMUNITY CENTER.

1930s: Aspiring ballerinas take a bow after a dance recital at the JCC.

1932: Sports activities drew many young people to the JCC. The basketball team shown here played in the city's athletic leagues. Coach Irving Tash stands in the back row on the left.

1937: Children run down the front steps of the JCC en route to a two-week trip to the JCC-sponsored Center Camp in Prince William County, Virginia.

As Washington's Jewish community diversified and grew, local Jews created organizations to serve those in need.

HELPING HANDS

1908: The Jewish Foster Home was formed by Minnie Goldsmith (center below), Rose Harmel, and Rudolph Behrend. In the first years, children were housed at The Friendly Inn on 6th Street, N.W. In 1911, the Foster Home purchased this house at 3213 Q Street in Georgetown. Children received secular education in public schools and Hebrew lessons at the Home.

1890: United Hebrew Charities was formed by several congregants at Washington Hebrew to help newly-arrived immigrants living downtown make "an economic, social, and cultural adjustment" to their new lives.

YEAR BOOK
OF THE
UNITED HEBREW
CHARITIES
OF THE DISTRICT OF COLUMBIA

1919-1920

1914: The Hebrew Home for the Aged was organized in 1914 when several Jewish businessmen learned that some homeless Jews were living in St. Elizabeths Hospital. This three-story brick building at 415 M Street, N.W., formerly home to the Young Men's Hebrew Association, became the first Hebrew Home. By 1925, the Home needed more space and built a new building at 1125 Spring Road, N.W.

The Hebrew Relief Society, formed in 1882, provided aid to Jews living in Southwest Washington. Nine businessmen donated $55 each in 1909 to start The Hebrew Free Loan Society and provide interest-free loans to immigrants. In 1921, the United Hebrew Relief Society provided baskets of food, coal, and other supplies to needy Jewish families throughout the city.

The Washington Council of Jewish Women
announces a
Kamouflage Karnival
THE OPENING GUN OF THE 1918-19 KAMPAIGN
FOR THE JEWISH WAR SUFFERERS

Patrons and Patronesses

THE COUNTESS OF READING
MRS. BERNARD BARUCH
MR. AND MRS. EMIL BERLINER
MRS. M. GOLDENBERG
REPRESENTATIVE AND MRS. JULIUS KAHN
MAJOR AND MRS. HERBERT LEHMAN
MR. AND MRS. EUGENE MEYER
MR. AND MRS. JULIUS ROSENWALD
REPRESENTATIVE ADOLPH J. SABATH
REPRESENTATIVE ISAAC SIEGEL
MR. AND MRS. ROGER STRAUS
MR. AND MRS. PAUL WARBURG
MR. AND MRS. MAURICE WERTHEIM
MR. AND MRS. SIMON WOLF

EIGHTH STREET TEMPLE
WEDNESDAY, MAY 1st, EIGHT P.M.

1930: Shown here are teachers at the Juanita K. [N...] Council House on 6th Stree[t] S.W., where Jewish immig[rant] children attended *cheder*. L to R: Rose Lewis (Glase[r], Myrtle Cohen, Edith Chidak[...] (Pascal), Ruth Glazer, Mary Lewis.

1895: In its early years, the Washington Chapter of the National Council of Jewish Women conducted an after-school recreation program for poor Jewish children in Southwest. During World War I, the chapter entertained soldiers and held events like a Kamouflage Karnival to raise funds for war relief.

ATTENTION, YEWS AND YOURS!

Men, Wives, Affinities, Sweethearts, Mothers-in-Law, Husbands, Soldiers, Lawyers, Doctors, Merchants and Gentlemen,

"Pack Up Your Troubles in Your Old Kit Bag"

and go ye, everybody, to the great

PACKAGE CAMOUFLAGE
AT THE
Temple of the Washington Hebrew Congregation
ON THE EVENING OF
WEDNESDAY, MAY 1st, AT 8 O'CLOCK

The Council of Jewish Women is no grafter,
But from each of you a package is what they are after.

Yes; bring a package containing "two quarters' worth," or "a hundred's worth!"

Be like Juliette on the spot,
With your package tied tight as a wedding knot,
Fling it in the basket, we ask no more,
And get a smile from the Guardian Angel at the door.

These packages will be auctioned by a "two-wise" auctioneer, who was passed by the National Board of Censors.

ALL PROCEEDS GO TO THE
JEWISH WAR SUFFERERS

Your presence and your presents at this affair
Means clothing and food for our brothers "over there."

A PROGRAM HAS BEEN ARRANGED that will not only tickle the ticklish, but will tickle the groucho.

"Prepare for an Evening of Hilarity."

NO ADMISSION. (God Forbid.)

Just bring a "package," every blessed one,
And we will guarantee you "bundles" of fun.
At close after you will have no time to knit,
Just come with a package and "do your bit."

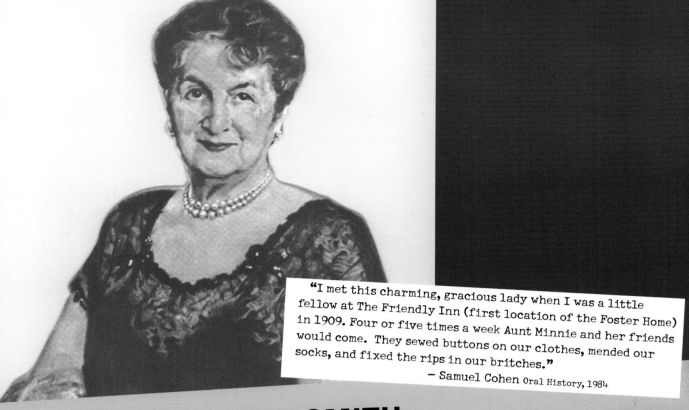

> "I met this charming, gracious lady when I was a little fellow at The Friendly Inn (first location of the Foster Home) in 1909. Four or five times a week Aunt Minnie and her friends would come. They sewed buttons on our clothes, mended our socks, and fixed the rips in our britches."
> — Samuel Cohen Oral History, 1984

MINNIE LANSBURGH GOLDSMITH (1871-1971) A LIFE OF SERVICE

Daughter of department store owner Gustav Lansburgh, Minnie Lansburgh Goldsmith became synonymous with Jewish philanthropy in Washington. She organized her first fundraising event at age 18—an evening of entertainment to raise money for the victims of the 1889 flood in Johnstown, Pennsylvania. Ever the hands-on activist, she entertained that evening by playing the banjo and zither.

In 1906, Goldsmith served as president of the United Hebrew Charities, working to improve the lives of impoverished families. As president of the local section of the National Council of Jewish Women in 1909, she oversaw the establishment of children's clubs. She led fundraising efforts for the Jewish Foster Home and the Hebrew Home for the Aged. In 1929, she helped create Washington's Community Chest, predecessor to the United Way. When the children at the Foster Home began to call her "Aunt Minnie," the name stuck.

On her 81st birthday, Minnie Goldsmith was honored by the Ladies Auxiliary of the Hebrew Home for the Aged. She admires the program with Blanche K. Alloy (left) and Marian Levy (right).

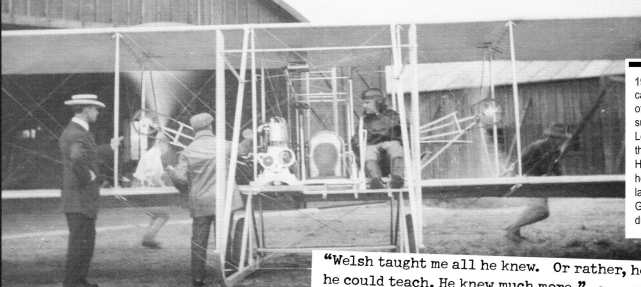

1912: Welsh (with his back to the camera) checking on the engine of the Wright C flyer prior to a successful test flight. Lieutenant Leighton Hazelhurst is seated in the plane, and Lieutenant Henry H. "Hap" Arnold (to Welsh's left) holds the strut of the plane. Arnold later became the Commanding General of the Army Air Forces during World War II.

"Welsh taught me all he knew. Or rather, he taught me all he could teach. He knew much more."– General Henry H. Arnold, 1949

ARTHUR WELSH (1881-1912) AMERICA'S FIRST JEWISH AVIATOR

Born in Russia, Laibel Wellcher immigrated with his family to Philadelphia and moved to Washington as a teen. His mother ran a grocery store in their home at 900 G Street, S.W. When he enlisted in the U.S. Navy in 1901, Wellcher changed his name to Arthur Welsh. His marriage to Anna Harmel in 1907 was the first wedding in Adas Israel's new synagogue at 6th and I Streets, N.W.

After watching Orville Wright's flight demonstrations at Fort Myer, Virginia, in 1909, Welsh joined the Wright brothers' first training class. A skilled pilot, Welsh trained many of America's first aviators.

In 1912, Welsh was killed in a crash at the College Park airfield during a test flight on a new military plane. He was buried in the Adas Israel cemetery in southeast Washington.

All present were in tears including Mr. Orville Wright and his sister who were doing all they could to console the mother and wife of the deceased.

Yiddish newspaper *Forward*, June 1912

1912: The Wright brothers sent Welsh to College Park, Maryland, to test a new military plane—the Wright C. On June 11, accompanied by Lieutenant Leighton Hazelhurst, Welsh flew a final test. Carrying a heavy load, the plane climbed just 200 feet before crashing into a field of daisies. Both men were killed instantly.

SHAPING THE DREAM

By the early 1900s, members of Washington's Jewish community were already working toward the dream of a Jewish homeland.

1910: This Jewish New Year's card depicts a Daughter of Zion carrying the Zionist banner. The inscription reads *L'shana tova tickatavu* (Happy New Year). Daughter of Zion chapters evolved into Hadassah, the women's Zionist organization founded by Henrietta Szold in 1912. Washington's first Hadassah chapter formed in 1919, soon after Szold visited the city.

"If you will it, it is not a dream."

Zionism founder
Theodor Herzl, 1896

European and Russian Jews had begun fleeing anti-Semitism and violent *pogroms* in the late 1800s. A small group made *aliyah* (immigration to Palestine). As conditions worsened during the early 20th century, increasing numbers settled there.

During World War I, Great Britain's Balfour Declaration announced support for a Jewish homeland in Palestine. In December 1917, the British captured Jerusalem, ending 400 years of Turkish rule. In Washington, a crowd celebrated on Christmas morning at the Belasco Theater on Lafayette Square. Local chapters of Zionist organizations raised money for Jewish settlement in Palestine.

1917: Members of the Washington Poale (Labor) Zion Society, including Morris Freilicoff (upper left) and his wife Sofie (bottom row, third from left), were photographed with visitor Yitzhak Ben-Zvi (second row, center). Ben-Zvi later became the second president of Israel.

Coins collected in these Jewish National Fund "blue boxes" helped purchase land for Jewish settlement in Palestine.

1926: Orthodox Zionists met with President Calvin Coolidge at the White House.

1930s–1940s

MEMORIES OF HORROR AND TRIUMPH

These two decades brought drastic changes worldwide—the ravages of the Great Depression, World War II, the near-destruction of European Jewry, and the struggle to secure and rebuild a Jewish homeland.

Washington also changed radically. The New Deal's influx of government workers brought new voices, skills, and geographic diversity to Washington's Jewish community. The horrifying extent of the Holocaust and the fight for a Jewish state forged a more cohesive community.

1942: Gunners manned DC rooftops in view of the Capitol. (background image)

1936: Nehemiah Cohen and Samuel Lehrman chose Washington for their new business venture, hoping federal workers would provide a strong market even during the Depression. Their first Giant supermarket opened at Georgia Avenue and Park Road, N.W., (below) in the midst of a snowstorm.

At right, Giant cashiers await their customers.

The stock market crash of 1929 ushered in the Great Depression, but Roosevelt's New Deal created thousands of new government jobs and helped ease hardships in Washington.

"Although you saw apple sellers on the street corners, you didn't see them like the rest of the country."
— Isabelle Gichner Oral History, 1980

"All we cared about was the government. We thought we were saving our system of democracy."
— Joseph Rauh Interview, 1989

GREAT DEPRESSION AND NEW DEAL

1945: Luna Ereza Diamond worked as secretary to Congressman Clinton P. Anderson (New Mexico), shown here. Her father, Sol Ereza, was a Sephardic immigrant and spiritual leader of the Sephardic community in Washington in the 1920s. Diamond continued to work with Anderson when he became Secretary of Agriculture and later a U.S. Senator.

Many small Jewish-owned businesses struggled with the economic downturn of the Depression. Some closed; some carried customers on credit. Jewish charitable organizations helped those in need. The United Hebrew Relief Society expanded its mission and employed professional social workers, becoming the Jewish Social Service Agency in 1933.

Newly-created federal government jobs spurred the arrival in droves of liberal Jewish men and women. The children of immigrant parents who had come to the U.S. to escape oppression, they were ideal candidates to help develop and implement social reform laws.

1933: After graduating from the Wharton School, economist Robert Nathan joined the Department of Commerce and worked on the first estimates of national income rates. In the 1940s, he served on the Planning Committee of the War Production Board and later in the Office of War Mobilization and Reconversion.

1931: As penniless Jewish men arrived in search of work, Anna Shulman and others founded the Hebrew Sheltering Society. The Society provided kosher meals, a change of clothes, and lodging.

1935: Clara Goldberg, a Radcliffe alumna from Boston, took the first civil service exam for college graduates. She then moved to Washington, where she could earn more money and find more interesting work than in her hometown. Soon after President Roosevelt signed the Social Security Act, she started her career at the new Social Security Board.

1935: Joseph Rauh was one of many Jewish New Dealers recruited by Harvard law professor Felix Frankfurter to help shape New Deal policies and programs. After clerking for Supreme Court Justices Benjamin Cardozo and Felix Frankfurter, he worked in the Department of Labor. Following his wartime service, he became a prominent civil rights lawyer in Washington.

1938: This annual report for the Jewish Social Service Agency shows expenses for refugee assistance, social workers, and the Jewish Foster Home.

September 26, 1930: The first issue of *The National Jewish Ledger*, a local Jewish newspaper, featured a New Year's message from President Herbert Hoover.

1932: Milton S. Kronheim opened his first liquor store at 3218 M Street, N.W., in 1903. After working as a bail bondsman during Prohibition, he returned to the liquor business in 1932 and became the largest wholesale distributor in the area. Here, Kronheim (seen standing in front of the boxes on the left) makes a wine delivery to Union Station.

1942: War Bond rally

WINDS OF WAR

1938: Arthur Bogner, a rabbi and psychiatrist who studied under Sigmund Freud, fled from Vienna to Washington. Prohibited from bringing his wife and children to the U.S. until he had a job, he was quickly employed by Ezras Israel Congregation, where he served as rabbi for the next 40 years.

1939: Alexandria's Beth El Hebrew Congregation obtained a visa for Rabbi Hugo Schiff of Karlsruhe, Germany, who had been imprisoned in Dachau. Schiff brought with him a Torah scroll saved from the Nazis. Rabbi Schiff and his wife became naturalized citizens on D-Day, 1944.

As events in Europe worsened, Washington Jews responded in many ways. Some organized rallies, wrote telegrams, and helped German Jewish refugees.

Hitler's annexation of Austria in 1938 (the *Anschluss*) heightened the fears of world Jewry. Many believed Palestine was the only refuge for European Jews. In D.C., the Jewish community organized an interdenominational meeting and sent thousands of telegrams to President Franklin Roosevelt urging that the doors of Palestine be kept open.

Nevertheless, a year later, Great Britain issued the "White Paper," severely restricting immigration to Palestine. Shortly after, World War II began. Washington Jews raised funds, petitioned the government for visas for those abroad, and helped newly-arrived refugees find jobs.

1939: The Women's Auxiliary of B'nai B'rith Argo Lodge raised money on behalf of Jewish refugees in Europe. Shown here is founder Frances Gewirz (seated at left) looking on as First Lady Eleanor Roosevelt addresses an Argo Lodge anniversary luncheon.

> "We, the undersigned, respectfully petition you, Mr. President...to intercede with the British government to keep open the gates of the Holy Land."
>
> Telegram sent to President Franklin D. Roosevelt, October 1938

October 23, 1938: 4,000 Washingtonians packed Constitution Hall to pressure the British government *not* to restrict Jewish immigration to Palestine. Organizers called the gathering a "mass meeting" rather than a "protest" because of sensitivity to the British government.

1942: Scrap metal drive

MASS MEETING
Support Of Jewish Rights
CONSTITUTION HALL
(18th and D Sts. N. W.)

Sunday Eve., 8 P. M.   October 23, 1938

"KEEP DOORS OF PALESTINE OPEN AS REFUGE FOR JEWS DRIVEN FROM EUROPEAN COUNTRIES"

Meeting called by Washington Emergency Refugee Committee as part of a Nation-wide Mass Meeting on Sunday, October 23, to present publicly the case of the Jewish People and their rights in Palestine.

. . Program . .

Speakers Include:
Senator George L. Radcliffe, Maryland
Congressman Hamilton Fish, New York
Dr. Peter Marshall, N. Y. Ave. Presbyterian Church
Chas. Edward Russell, Liberal and Publicist
Mgr. Francis J. Hass, Dean of the School Social Science, Catholic University
Dr. Abram Simon, Washington Hebrew Congregation
Rabbi Isadore Breslau, Chairman

We must show our strength - - - <u>You Must Attend</u> The Meeting for the eyes of the nation are on <u>Wash-ington</u> as the Capital of the United States.

NO ADMISSION

E. I. KAUFMANN, Chairman
Emergency Committee

1941: Ben Aaronson of the Jewish War Veterans pulls a lottery number during an early draft pick at the American Legion Building in Washington.

JEWISH MEN AND WOMEN IN UNIFORM

Washington Jews — men and women — served valiantly on all fronts of World War II.

1945: Staff Sergeant Morton Brodofsky (Brody) of the 1st Armored Division was awarded a Silver Star for actions in Artena, Italy. The citation states: "…completely disregarding his own personal safety, Sgt. Brodofsky voluntarily took up a new position… Seeing Brodofsky's action, most of the men returned to their positions and inflicted a major defeat on the enemy."

1945: Fay Shulman enlisted as a WAVE (Women Accepted for Voluntary Emergency Service). "I would come home every night…and see in the newspaper a name that either I knew or went to school with," she remembers. "It began to hit home." After hospital training, she was assigned to Bremerton Naval Hospital in Washington state.

1944: Major Frank Rich served 27 months in the Far East in the Army Air Forces as Deputy Chief of Staff of the Statistical Control Office. "Conditions were very primitive—no air-conditioning, a crate for a desk," he remembers. "Dangerous air missions flew without radar. I made sure they did not run out of fuel."

Within a week after Japan bombed Pearl Harbor on December 7, 1941, the U.S. was at war with Japan, Germany, and Italy. Members of Washington's Jewish community joined every branch of the military.

With the country engaged in both Atlantic and Pacific theaters of combat, Washington became arguably the most important city in the world. Temporary buildings rose overnight to house new war agencies. Thousands of educated Jewish men and women, many the first in their families to graduate from college, flocked to Washington to work in the war effort.

1944: Private William Mann was captured by the German Army during the Battle of the Bulge. "I had no idea what was in store for American Jewish prisoners . . . I punched my fist down into a snowbank and took my dog tags off and dropped them in there . . . and from that time on I was a 'Catholic.'" Mann survived 106 days in a prisoner of war camp near Frankfurt, Germany.

WESTERN UNION

WP176 28 GOVT=WUX WASHINGTON DC 20 523P
MRS BEATRICE BRODOFOSKY=
3128 M ST NORTHWEST=

544 OCT 20 PM 6 05

REGRET TO INFORM YOU YOUR SON PRIVATE MORTON BRODOFOSKY WAS SLIGHTLY WOUNDED IN ACTION THIRTY SEPTEMBER IN ITALY YOU WILL BE ADVISED AS REPORTS OF CONDITION ARE RECEIVED=
J A ULIO THE ADJUTANT GENERAL.

1942: At home on leave, Corporal Sidney Hais posed with his mother Ida Flax Hais in front of the family grocery store at 7th and C Street, N.E.

1942: A Passover *seder* held at the Willard Hotel drew over 1,000 soldiers, friends, and family.

1942: Agudas Achim Congregation in Alexandria loaned a Torah to the Marine Corps based in Quantico, Virginia.

ON THE HOME FRONT

AWARD
TO THE EMPLOYEES OF THE
FRED. S. GICHNER IRON WORKS
INCORPORATED
WASHINGTON, D. C.

1943: After America entered the war, Gichner Ironworks converted to producing war materials. When the company received an award for exceptional efficiency and production, Henry Gichner said: "Let's keep right on going until we get the V-Flag for Victory!"

In and around Washington, the Jewish community supported the war in a variety of ways.

I AM AN AMERICAN DAY
EXERCISES AND
WAR BOND RALLY
Under Joint Auspices of the
ADAS ISRAEL SISTERHOOD
AND BROTHERHOOD
Wednesday, May 23rd, 1945
at 8:15 P.M.
at the Synagogue

In support of the war effort, local Jews joined their fellow citizens in rationing sugar, butter, and coffee. They recycled newspapers, bobby pins, and cigarette wrappers. They housed soldiers and civilian newcomers in extra rooms.

The Jewish War Veterans' Washington Post No. 58 and the Jewish Welfare Board sponsored High Holiday services and Passover *seders* for military personnel. The Jewish Community Center provided housing references to thousands of newly arrived "government girls" through a Room Registry. The JCC offered a full program of activities, including daytime jitterbug contests for nighttime shift workers. Its policy was: "Your uniform is your admission to all activities and facilities."

"...a colonel asked me if I would like to sell all of my poultry to the U.S. Army...My chicken went to our soldiers who were located all over the world...Boys from Washington, D.C., wrote me letters thanking me for the good poultry they received."

— Fred Kolker   Oral History, 1985

1942: Phyllis Hagedorn Cohen joined the Middle East Division of the Foreign Economic Administration. She was the only Jewish staff member at her agency.

1940s: Fred Kolker (center) ran a poultry business at 1263 4th Street, N.E. He is shown here with Cantor and *shochet* (ritual butcher) Moshe Yoelson, entertainer Al Jolson's father.

1942: Roselyn Silverman moved from Portsmouth, Virginia during the war to work for the Navy Department. She is shown here in her room at Dissin's Guest House, a boarding house catering to young Jews at 2013 Massachusetts Avenue, N.W. Severe housing shortages forced many war workers to share scarce rooms in boarding houses and private homes across the city.

1940s: Many local organizations sponsored rallies, soldiers' dances, and other events in support of the war. The sisterhood of Washington Hebrew hosted USO dances like this one.

GOVERNMENT OF THE DISTRICT OF COLUMBIA

HEREBY PRESENTS TO

ELIZABETH C. HIRSHMAN

THIS CERTIFICATE OF RECOGNITION FOR PATRIOTISM AND UNSELFISHNESS IN SERVING CIVILIAN DEFENSE IN THE DISTRICT OF COLUMBIA DURING WORLD WAR II.

GIVEN AT WASHINGTON, DISTRICT OF COLUMBIA, THIS *1st* DAY OF *November*, ONE THOUSAND NINE HUNDRED AND FORTY-FOUR.

1944: Elizabeth Hirshman received this certificate of recognition for her service as an air raid warden in Washington's civil defense program. Wardens patrolled the streets, directing people to air raid shelters and ensuring that blackouts were observed.

WASHINGTON JEWISH YOUTH FEDERATION

YOUTH RALLY AND DANCE

FIRST AID
MOTOR CORPS
AIR RAID TRAINING
BLOOD BANKS

PHYSICAL FITNESS
DEFENSE JOBS
MESSENGER SERVICE
ARMY & NAVY WORK

What Can You Do For

CIVILIAN DEFENSE?

- Mary K. Browne
- Major Kelly
- Chief Murphy
- Community Singing

Music By The "RHYTHM MAKERS" - 12 pieces
THURSDAY, FEB. 3, 1942 8 P.M.
JEWISH COMMUNITY CENTER

YOU CAN HELP CRUSH HITLER NOW

and stop the mass murder of
your brethren in Hitler's Europe

★ ★ ★

BACK THE ATTACK — BUY WAR BONDS

EIG'S LIQUOR STORE
WASHINGTON, D. C.

THE DISTRICT LEADER

"FOLLOW THE LEADER — — — THE DISTRICT LEADER"
Volume 3—No. 15   WASHINGTON, D. C., OCTOBER 29, 1941   Subscription—$1.50 Yearly

WERE YOU AT THE AIR-RAID RALLY?

The Air You Breathe Is FREE — But Will It Always Be Free of BOMBS?

1940s: Victor Perlmutter published and edited *The District Leader*, a bi-weekly local newspaper for residents of Southeast Washington.

Are we immune from bombs and destruction?

It can't happen. It won't happen. But don't tempt fate. Bombs know no discrimination.

You believe the security of your home is your air-raid shelter?

It can shelter you only as securely as you've built it. Merely locking the door is not enough.

Wake up, citizens. Don't be so smug because we are Americans. Being an American is miraculous. But our good fairy will turn into a monster if we wear out her magic wand and only make demands, giving nothing in return.

The best way to avoid disaster is to be prepared to face it.

Of course this mass attendance of the citizens groups, the clergy, and various organizations, was just a preliminary gathering to appoint air raid wardens, their assistants and members of executive committees on civilian defense. You didn't want to be one anyway! Because this job entails a great deal of work and study and obligation.

But let the bombs come, and those who were appointed will suddenly become your saviors. You will seek them for safety, for comfort, for advice. And they will be waiting, prepared and willing to help you.

For there are always a few who, thank God, can look forward and see wisdom in preparedness; who are glad to help their fellowmen who were not so wise and

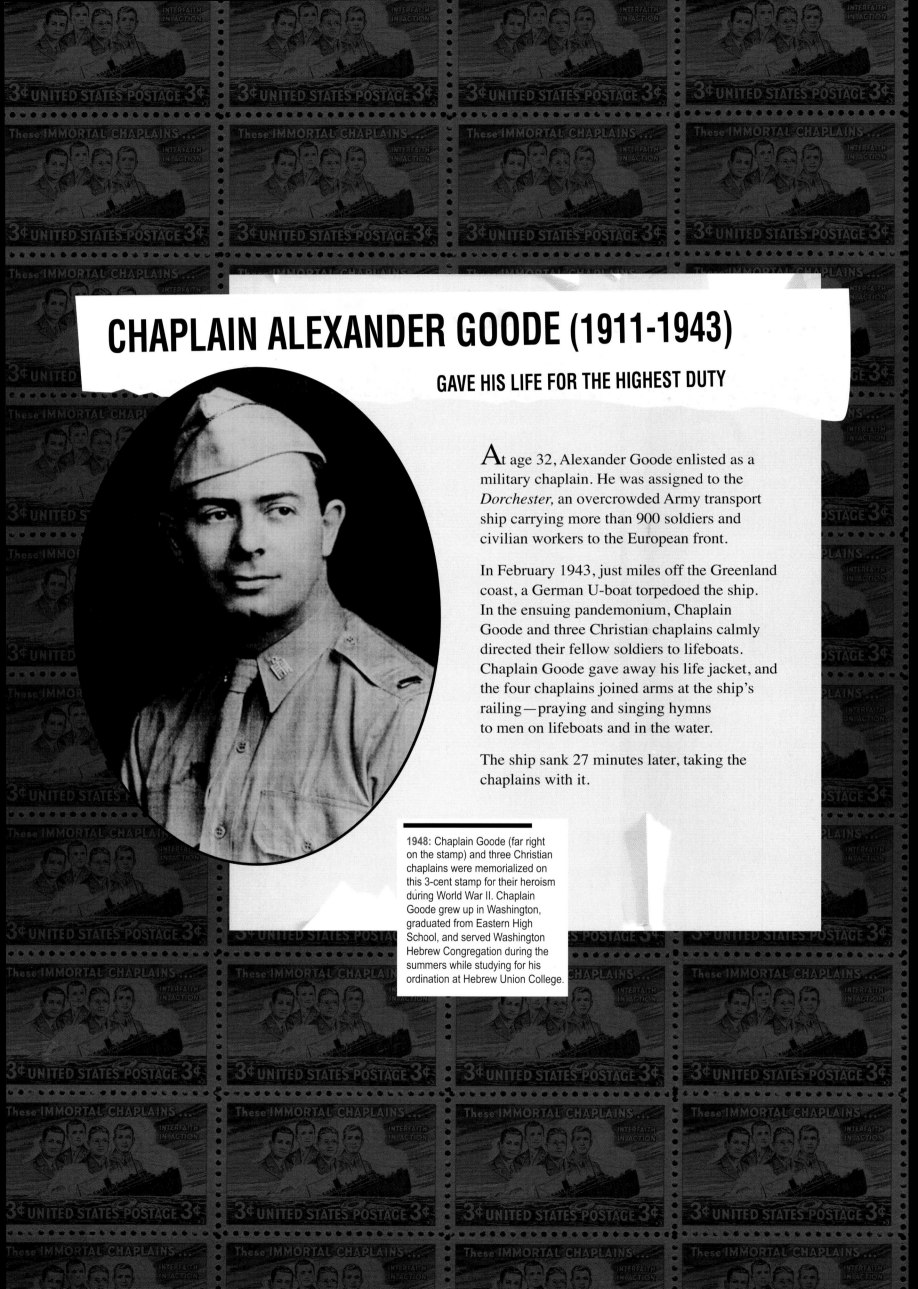

CHAPLAIN ALEXANDER GOODE (1911-1943)

GAVE HIS LIFE FOR THE HIGHEST DUTY

At age 32, Alexander Goode enlisted as a military chaplain. He was assigned to the *Dorchester,* an overcrowded Army transport ship carrying more than 900 soldiers and civilian workers to the European front.

In February 1943, just miles off the Greenland coast, a German U-boat torpedoed the ship. In the ensuing pandemonium, Chaplain Goode and three Christian chaplains calmly directed their fellow soldiers to lifeboats. Chaplain Goode gave away his life jacket, and the four chaplains joined arms at the ship's railing—praying and singing hymns to men on lifeboats and in the water.

The ship sank 27 minutes later, taking the chaplains with it.

1948: Chaplain Goode (far right on the stamp) and three Christian chaplains were memorialized on this 3-cent stamp for their heroism during World War II. Chaplain Goode grew up in Washington, graduated from Eastern High School, and served Washington Hebrew Congregation during the summers while studying for his ordination at Hebrew Union College.

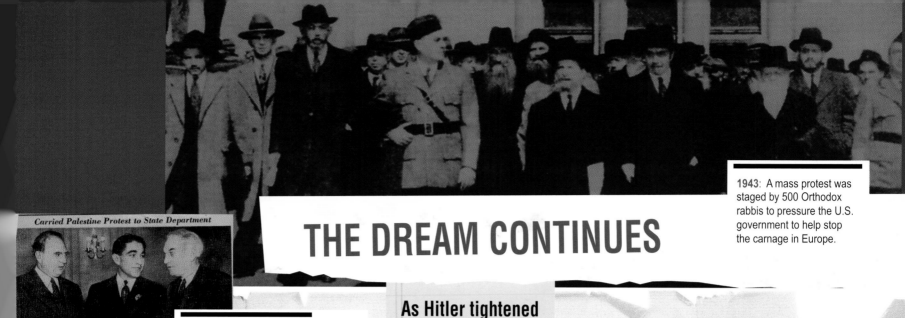

THE DREAM CONTINUES

1943: A mass protest was staged by 500 Orthodox rabbis to pressure the U.S. government to help stop the carnage in Europe.

Carried Palestine Protest to State Department

Protesting the new British policy in Palestine, these Jewish lead...

1939: National Jewish leaders met with Secretary of State Cordell Hull to protest British policy in Palestine. Present (left to right) were Judge Morris Rothenberg, Chairman of the Council of Jewish Agencies for Palestine; Rabbi Isadore Breslau, Director of the American Zionist Bureau; and Rabbi Solomon Goldman, National President of ZOA.

As Hitler tightened his grip on Europe, local Zionist leaders worked diligently to build support for a Jewish homeland.

Like American Jews in general, Washington Jews held differing views about Zionism. Many were early supporters of a Jewish homeland, but few belonged to Zionist organizations. Leaders of the Washington chapter of the Zionist Organization of America (ZOA) worked to change this situation. They organized a flurry of activities at local synagogues, homes of prominent members of the community, and the Jewish Community Center.

Local Zionists—like Edmund I. Kaufmann, head of Kay Jewelry, and Rabbi Isadore Breslau, director of the American Zionist Bureau's lobbying efforts—rose to prominence on Washington's national stage.

March 10, 1942

Jewish Community Council
Executive Committee Meeting

A special meeting of the Executive Committee of the Washington Jewish Community Council was held Tuesday, night, March 10th in the Board Room of the Jewish Community Center. Mr. Hymen Goldman was in the Chair.

The following members were present:

Rabbi Isadore Breslau, Mrs. Isadore Breslau, Mr. Zalman Henkin, Mrs. Lawrence Koenigsberger, Rabbi Solomon Metz, Mr. Chas. Pilser, Mr. John Safer, Rabbi Henry Segal, Mr. Isidore Turover, and Mr. Aaron Goldman, **Joseph Barr.**

In all instances, the absences of other members was explained because of the short notice which preceded the meeting.

The Chairman announced that the sole purpose of the meeting was to determine what action the Executive Committee wished to take regarding the tragic "Struma" incident.

Rabbi Breslau related the facts of the case—

The "S. S. Struma," an unseaworthy boat, crowded with 750 Roumanian refugees, was not permitted to land in Turkey because the Palestine High Commissioner refused to issue the necessary certificates. The boat, forced to leave Turkey, went to pieces shortly thereafter, and all but six or seven drowned. The British War Cabinet then expressly certified and approved the action taken by its High Commissioner.

Rabbi Breslau stated that it was his feeling that some type of action was called for, but that he was not sure that a protest meeting would accomplish the desired results. He felt that any public controversy between the Jews and the British government would be seized upon by our enemies and exploited as a sign of division between the democracies. He further stated that our protests, if any, should be directed against the British Colonial Office and not against the British government. However, he did not feel that such a fine distinction would be recognized by the general public if a public protest meeting were held. He suggested that perhaps the same ends could be attained by calling a meeting or meetings which could be designated as a "Memorial" meeting.

Mr. Lawrence Koenigsberger stated that she was absolutely against any type of protest meeting. She emphasized the fact that we are at war and the the times were not propitious for a protest meeting against the actions of the British government, no matter how emotionally moved we were by the tragic fate of the 750 innocent people.

...uld be accepted by the Council at its meeting on March 1...
...of the Council. The Chairman expressly stated that the...
...lutions drafted in advance was simply to expedite the c...
...and did not bind the Council from taking any other acti...
preferable.

...iscussion on certain arbitration matters which the Chair...
...th Mr. Lawrence Koenigsberger.

...er business, the meeting was closed.

Respectfully submitted,

Aaron Goldman
Secretary

1942: The Jewish Community Council of Greater Washington agonized over a fitting response to the *S.S. Struma* tragedy. The British had refused entry to Palestine for the 767 Romanian refugees on board. When the ship broke apart, all but one drowned. Unable to act unanimously, the Council resolved that memorial services could be held at synagogues, but protests would be inappropriate. Chairman Hymen Goldman (above left), upset at the Council's discord, left the meeting in tears. His son, Aaron Goldman (above right), recorded the minutes of the meeting.

Notice of Mass Protest Meeting . . . Prominent Speakers . . . Everyone Invited
MAYFLOWER HOTEL, Thursday, July 11, 8:00 P. M.
Meeting Jointly Sponsored by The American Christian-Palestine Committee and the Jewish Community Council.

THE JEWISH COMMUNITY COUNCIL OF WASHINGTON, D. C.

Zion Officials Installed

1930s-1941: The Kalorama apartment of Supreme Court Justice Louis D. Brandeis served as a salon for national and local Zionist leaders. When Justice Brandeis died in 1941, the local chapter of the Zionist Organization of America changed its name to the Louis D. Brandeis District of Washington, D.C.

1940: Left to right: Rabbi Isadore Breslau and Louis Spiegler, President of the local chapter of the ZOA, toast Edmund Kaufmann, the organization's new national President.

OFFICIAL PROGRAM

"WE WILL NEVER DIE"
A Mass Memorial Dedicated to the Two Million Jewish Dead of Europe
Constitution Hall • Washington, D.C. • April 12, 1943

1943: Activist Peter Bergson's lobby groups worked to build popular sympathy for the plight of European Jews. The Emergency Committee to Save the Jewish People of Europe sponsored newspaper ads calling attention to the Holocaust, and staged a pageant memorializing the massacre of Jews. First Lady Eleanor Roosevelt, several Supreme Court Justices, and members of the international diplomatic corps were among the thousands who saw the pageant, *We Will Never Die*, at Constitution Hall.

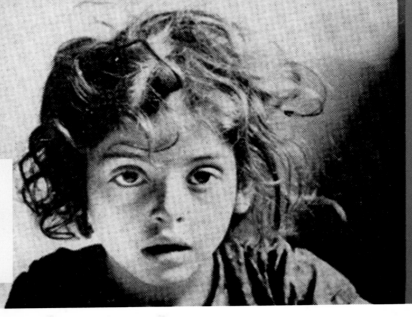

My Pledge For Youth Aliyah

I MAKE MY PLEDGE FOR $_____
to Hadassah for Youth Aliyah

SAVING THE CHILDREN

TREASURY DEPARTMENT
WASHINGTON
January 16, 1943

DEFENSE SAVINGS STAFF

Mrs. Raphael Tourover
4812 30th Street, Northwest
Washington, D. C.

My dear Mrs. Tourover:

    Your letter about the children in Teheran came as a real tonic. I cannot tell you how happy I am that the children now really seem to be safely on their way to Palestine.

    As you know, I think that the National Youth Aliyah is doing a great humanitarian piece of work for these bewildered children bereft of their own homes, and is bringing them back to a healthy, useful life in Palestine. I am therefore happy to pledge the $480 which will defray the expenses for one child for two years. I understand that I can give this sum over a period of two years, and I will therefore send you the amount from time to time.

    I hope that your meeting will be most successful.

    With best wishes,

    Sincerely yours,

    Elinor F. Morgenthau
    (Mrs.

As the war raged, Jewish women in the Washington area struggled to help children at risk.

Founded in 1933, Youth Aliyah rescued Jewish children from increasing danger in Europe and brought them to safety in Palestine. There, Hadassah—the Women's Zionist Organization—assumed responsibility for the youngsters' housing and schooling in special children's villages on *kibbutzim* (cooperative farms).

In Washington, a number of women lobbied and raised funds for the children. Denise Tourover, Hadassah's first Washington representative, worked tirelessly to rescue the "Tehran children"—700 Polish orphans stranded in Persia after making their way out of Europe. She pleaded with State Department officials and ambassadors until British ships finally transported the children to Palestine.

HADASSAH AIDS YOUTH ALIYAH MOVEMENT

1943: L to R: Lillian Offenberg, local Hadassah president, Gisela Warburg, National Youth Aliyah chairman, Denise Tourover. Denise Tourover worked on the most famous Youth Aliyah project: the rescue of the "Tehran children." In the letter above, Elinor Morgenthau, wife of the Secretary of the Treasury, expressed relief about the children's rescue.

MRS. EDWARD CAFRITZ

BROADCAST

ON

"YOUTH ALIYAH"

WINX

SUNDAY - 6:30 P.M.

FEBRUARY, 18

1945: Mildred Cafritz used her radio show on WINX and her influence as chair of Hadassah's local Youth Aliyah Committee to appeal for funds for refugee children. By March 1945, her committee had raised $33,000 for housing, education, and vocational training.

1947: Sally Kravette (right) became chair of Youth Aliyah for Northern Virginia after hearing Denise Tourover speak. She remembers: "My quota was $4,000. I raised $7,000 that year."

GIV'AT WASHINGTON

1946: With the help of others, Rabbi Zemach Green (right) established Giv'at Washington, a school and home for orphaned survivors in Palestine.

RELIEF AND RESCUE AFTER THE WAR

1946: Captain Herbert Fierst (right), is awarded a Legion of Merit Award by General John H. Hilldring for his work for the "care and repatriation of the millions of displaced persons." Fierst worked closely with Hilldring, Assistant Secretary for Occupied Areas, at the State Department.

Joy over the war's end was clouded by news of the murder of six million Jews. The local community worked to save the remnants of European Jewry.

American Jews were shocked by the world's seeming disregard for Holocaust survivors who remained behind barbed wire in DP (Displaced Persons) camps in Europe. By now a majority of American Jews were convinced of the urgent need for a Jewish state. Washingtonians mobilized a grassroots campaign.

Women's organizations raised money and collected food and medical supplies for DPs. At the Pentagon and later the State Department, Herbert Fierst helped DPs gain access to the U.S. Occupation Zone in Europe. Meanwhile, the United Jewish Appeal stepped up fundraising to support immigration to Palestine.

> "At the end of World War II, my father couldn't look in the mirror to shave. He felt that if he had lifted one more finger, raised one more dollar, knocked on the door of one more Congressman, signed one more petition, maybe one more Jewish child would have been saved."
>
> Martin Kamerow Oral History, 1997

American Support Launched This Ship . . .

GIVE--and they live. DON'T--and they die.

WASHINGTON'S

National Women's Division
UNITED JEWISH APPEAL

UNITED JEWISH APPEAL

for $1,000,000

1946-48: Washington's United Jewish Appeal held—and met—its first million dollar campaign in 1946. The Women's Division of UJA raised over $250,000 in 1948.

BEN HECHT

1946: An illegal immigration operation known as *Aliyah Bet* smuggled groups of war refugees onto ships heading for Palestine. Peter Bergson's lobbying groups raised money to purchase and equip one such ship – the *S.S. Ben Hecht.*

Washingtonian Elihu Bergman (right) was held at a detention camp on Cyprus when his *Aliyah Bet* ship was captured by the British. Bergman was one of 250 American volunteers working on *Aliyah Bet* ships.

SECURING THE DREAM

Washington Jews played crucial roles – both clandestinely and publicly – to support creation of a Jewish state.

The Holocaust proved that Jews could not rely on world leaders to speak for them. When the allied nations met in 1945 to organize the United Nations, American Jews demanded inclusion. Jewish presence at the conference laid the groundwork for U.N. support of the plan to partition Palestine and create a Jewish state. Several Washingtonians influenced the 1947 U.N. vote to partition Palestine.

Local members of the clandestine Sonneborn Institute held secret meetings to raise money for a Jewish state and its underground army, the *Haganah*. Locally, Zionist youth groups such as Habonim prepared young Jews for future leadership.

1947: This sticker was used to protest the British troops who forced *Exodus 1947*, a ship carrying nearly 4,000 Jewish DPs, back to Germany. In Washington, Rabbis Solomon Metz (Adas Israel), Harry Silverstone (Tifereth Israel), and Henry Segal (B'nai Israel) marched on the British Embassy with Habonim leaders shouting "Let my people go!"

S. S. EXODUS 1947

BRITISH FLOATING DACHAU

1945: Washingtonian Edmund I. Kaufmann was among the 50 representatives selected by the Jewish Agency to speak for Zionists at the U.N. organizing conference in San Francisco. This letter to his grandsons describes his role in drafting a plan for Jewish settlement in Palestine.

1947: On November 29, 1947, the U.N. voted to partition Palestine into Jewish and Arab states. Washington Jews had worked tirelessly to assure the required two-thirds vote. Dr. Harvey Ammerman (above) convinced one of his patients serving at the Chilean embassy to intercede. The patient called Chile's ambassador to the U.N., and Chile abstained. While working as the physician at the Guatemalan embassy, Ammerman also won the backing of Guatemalan Ambassador Jorge Garcia Granados.

THE UNITED NATIONS CONFERENCE
ON INTERNATIONAL ORGANIZATION

437 Fairmont Hotel
San Francisco, Cal.
May 24, 1945

Dear Dick and Lee:

Your Pop has been here nearly a week. It has been most interesting and enlightening. My official standing is somewhat confusing, but regardless of this, I have been permitted to sit in nearly all of the conferences and committee meetings, most of them secret.

Before leaving Washington, I wrote a three-page letter regarding Palestine, and after discussing it with Oscar Cox, he boiled it down to slightly over a page. This memorandum is to be the basis of a memorandum to be submitted to the various Jewish organizations for approval. It is my personal opinion that it will be broad and fair enough to assure us that it will meet with their approval and subsequent endorsement. For the record, I am quoting this memorandum. The letter preceding it is in my files in Washington and was addressed to Drew Pearson. The following is the memorandum:

"Opportunity for Displaced Jews
of Europe to go to Palestine

"This is intended only as a very brief memorandum on the subject to bring out the major points in outline.

"No human beings in Europe or in all history have been persecuted as barbarically or moved about as have been the Jews by the Nazis.

"The Jews of Europe—particularly those who have been displaced—should justly have a reasonable and effective opportunity to go to Palestine if they wish.

"No German Jew, for example, who was moved to Poland for the lowest form of slave labor, should be forced to return only to Germany. That will be the only practical alternative unless steps are taken in the near future to give them a reasonable and effective opportunity to go to Palestine if they wish to do so. To afford such a reasonable and practicable opportunity, it will be necessary and desirable to:

THE UNITED NATIONS CONFERENCE
ON INTERNATIONAL ORGANIZATION

- 2 -

"1. Obtain a change in the limitations in the White Paper on the number of Jews that are authorized to go to Palestine and the time during which they can go.

"2. Make arrangements with UNRRA to move to Palestine the Jews who wish to go there and to feed and furnish them with their other vital needs until they reach Palestine.

"3. Provide adequate funds for those Jews who choose to go to Palestine so that they can effectively help themselves and be productive citizens in Palestine. This might be done through long-term non-interest bearing loans made out of a revolving fund. The revolving fund could be made up of reparation and restitution allowances and voluntary contributions. A well-documented claim should be filed soon with the Reparations Commission in Moscow for equitable restitution and reparations for the Jews. Consideration might also be given to requesting the U. S. Government to make available, on an equitable restitution or reparations principle, part of the German assets and funds which were recently found by U. S. forces in the salt mine in Germany. This would probably require legislation. Voluntary contributions might be sought at the same time the other two courses are being followed."

My plans of returning are rather vague. I am to go [to Los] Angeles within the next few days and will leave from [there] for Washington. I shall not leave, however, until I had talks with Governor Stassen, Senator Vandenberg [and C]ongressman Eaton.

The trip here was restful, and since my arrival I [have] been in bed nearly every night by 11 o'clock.

With best love to you and all of our dear ones,

Devotedly,

Pop

Messrs. Dick and Lee Kaufmann
4845 Colorado Avenue
Washington, D. C.

VOTING SHEET
UNITED NATIONS GENERAL ASSEMBLY

(au Parti Z'du T Palestine)

Saturday Nov. 29, 1947

Yes ___
NO ___
ABSTAIN ___
ABSENT ___

SUBJECT ___

	YES	NO	ABSTAIN	ABSENT			YES	NO	ABSTAIN	ABSENT
AFGHANISTAN						IRAQ				
ARGENTINA						LEBANON				
AUSTRALIA						LIBERIA				
BELGIUM						LUXEMBOURG				
BOLIVIA						MEXICO				
BRAZIL						NETHERLANDS				
BYELORUSSIA						NEW ZEALAND				
CANADA						NICARAGUA				
CHILE						NORWAY				
CHINA						PAKISTAN				
COLOMBIA						PANAMA				
COSTA RICA						PARAGUAY				
CUBA						PERU				
CZECHOSLOVAKIA						PHILL				
DENMARK						POLAND				
DOMINICAN R.						SAUDI				
ECUADOR						SIAM				
EGYPT						SWEDEN				
EL SALVADOR						SYRIA				
ETHIOPIA						TURKEY				
FRANCE										
GREECE										
GUATEMALA										
HAITI										
HONDURAS										
ICELAND										
INDIA										
IRAN						YEMEN				
						YUGOSLAVIA				
TOTAL						TOTAL				

Isador Turover recorded the results of the historic partition vote on this tally sheet.

1945-48: These Washington Jews undertook a massive fundraising campaign in secret to support the *Haganah* (underground Jewish army) in its war for independence. Men and women raised suitcases full of cash that provided ships and crew for *Aliyah Bet* (illegal immigration to Palestine), machinery for a munitions factory, and World War II surplus weapons and explosives for the *Haganah*.

Abraham Kay

Morris Pollin

Jacob Kamerow

Ruth Cherner

Theodore Herzl Levin

Joe Cherner

Isador Turover

Morris Rodman

Leo Bernstein

Hymen Goldman

"Before Israel was a state, we had many Haganah meetings. We were getting ready to help Jews get into Palestine. They needed money for guns, ammunition and ships. We met at my office at 718 5th Street."
— Leo Bernstein   Oral History, 1998

A DREAM COMES TRUE

On May 14, 1948, at midnight in Jerusalem, David Ben-Gurion proclaimed the independence of Israel. Eleven minutes later, at 6:11 p.m. in Washington, President Truman announced the United States' recognition of the Jewish state—helping to guarantee Jews worldwide a cultural home, and spiritual center.

Washington Jews celebrated with thanks and jubilation. An exuberant crowd gathered at the Jewish Agency building at 2210 Massachusetts Avenue, N.W., as the new flag was raised. They spilled out the door onto the lawn, singing, dancing, and praying.

1948: Members of the Zionist youth group Habonim danced the *hora* at the Washington celebration of the new State of Israel.

"We had a beautiful time. We cried and we danced and we cried. Oh, they must have had several hundred people in the street."

— Fannye Rose Oral History, 1981

1948: Arnold Kravette (back right) and fellow members of the Zionist Organization of America sterilize and repackage canned goods in a Falls Church DGS store for shipment to Israel.

BUILDING A NATION

As Israelis fought for independence, Washingtonians raised money, collected supplies, and lobbied for political support.

The United Jewish Appeal and other organizations worked tirelessly to help Israel meet overwhelming economic and social needs. Several Washingtonians joined other American Jewish leaders in pledging to help raise $1 billion to enable Israel to build infrastructure and absorb more immigrants. A committee composed of Leo Bernstein, Abraham Kay, Joseph Cherner, and Garfield Kass selected a suitable building for the new embassy at 22nd and R Streets, N.W.

Washington Zionists were also among those Americans to make *aliyah* (immigration to Israel).

1956: Fannie Simson, National Chairman of Sponsors of Israel Bonds, presents Celia Grossberg (left) with the first Woman of Valor award from Israel Bonds for her efforts to encourage investment in Israel.

1949: Carl and Doris Allentuck and daughter Leba were among the Washington Zionists to make *aliyah*. They are shown here at Moshav Bet Herut.

1950s: Ardent Zionist Nehemiah Cohen (right), co-founder of Giant Food, greets David Ben-Gurion.

1950s: Prominent Washington philanthropists Dorothy and Jack Bender (left) and Naomi and Nehemiah Cohen (right) are shown here with Minnie and Abraham Kay aboard ship en route to Israel in the 1950s.

1954: Seen here at an Israel Bonds dinner are, from left to right: Paul Himmelfarb, Abraham Kay, Robert A. Philipson, Joe Cherner, Henry Montor, I.S. Turover. Seated, left to right: unknown, Herbert S. Morrison, former deputy Prime Minister of Great Britain, Robert Nathan.

The work in Israel has only begun.
— Abraham S. Kay, 1949

1955: A leading philanthropist in Washington, Kay supported many projects in Israel, including this convalescent center in Naharia for disabled veterans.

1950: Washingtonian Abraham S. Kay (right and above) was one of 44 American Jews invited to Israel by Prime Minister David Ben-Gurion (left) to form the Development Corporation for Israel (now known as Israel Bonds).

1964: The Jewish National Fund dedicated the Abraham S. Kay Forest in Kay's memory in 1964. Minnie Kay is seen here on the right at the dedication ceremony.

ENTRANCE BEVERLEY BEACH CLUB
MEMBERSHIP LIMITED TO
GENTILES ONLY
LEASED AND OPERATED BY
BEVERLEY BEACH CLUB INC.
MAYO MD.

POSITIVELY NO DOGS PERMITTED

1950s: Washington Jews were confronted with this sign at popular vacation spots such as Beverley Beach on the South River near Annapolis. Turned away, they instead frequented nearby beaches such as Bay Ridge and Tivoli.

RESTRICTIONS

An undercurrent of anti-Semitism pervaded Jewish life in Washington.

None of said lands, interests therein or improvements thereon shall be sold, resold, conveyed, leased, rented to or in any way used, occupied or acquired by any person of Negro blood or to any person of the Semitic race, blood, or origin which racial description shall be deemed to include Armenians, Jews, Hebrews, Persians and Syrians.

1948: Discriminatory covenants included in deeds throughout the Washington area had barred the sale of property to Jews, blacks, and other minorities. In its 1948 *Shelley v. Kramer* decision, the Supreme Court ruled restrictive covenants in real estate unenforceable.

1935: After graduating from Cornell University Law School, Albert Arent declined a job offer from a New York law firm. "My name and my looks were ambiguous. I was to be their 'show Jew,'" he later recalled. Instead, he took a job in the federal government and joined the new Civil Liberties Unit of the U.S. Department of Justice in 1939. Arent left the government in l944, when his friend, Henry J. Fox, who was also Jewish, offered him a job in his new law firm. The D.C. law firm Arent Fox was born.

For many years, downtown department stores like Woodward & Lothrop did not hire Jews. Jewish physicians were barred from holding office in the Medical Society of Washington. Builders used restrictive covenants and real estate agents advertised new houses "near churches" to dissuade Jews from buying property in neighborhoods like Spring Valley and parts of Chevy Chase, Maryland.

Jewish responses to these restrictions took many forms. Argo Lodge of B'nai B'rith formed a Vaudeville Vigilance committee in 1916 to watch for anti-Semitic content in theaters. Washington Jewish physicians formed the Jacobi Medical Society in 1926. Woodmont and Indian Spring Country Clubs provided social outlets and leisure activities for Jewish families. Neighborhoods such as Forest Hills were not restricted and became predominantly Jewish in the 1940s and 1950s.

Following World War II, restrictions gradually eased.

I went to a high school (Business High School) which had a lot of Jewish kids. At football games, kids from the other schools would shout "Izzy, Ikey, Jakey, Sam, We're the boys who eat no ham! Business! Business!" It was no joke. We resented it.

Robert I. Silverman   Oral History, 1981

I applied at the telephone company [in 1921], and if I had put on the application that I was Jewish I could never have gotten the job. They didn't employ Jews.
Ethel Wool Kagen   Interview, 2000

When I graduated from Central High School in 1938, I wanted to go into journalism. I was told not to apply for a job at the *Evening Star* as they already had one Jewish reporter and were not likely to hire more. I went to Shirley Povich at *The Washington Post*, and he hired me at 25 cents an inch of published material.

Gershon Fishbein   Interview, 2005

I was first in my George Washington University Law School graduating class in 1950. I was accepted at a leading firm. "We don't mind hiring Jews," they told me. "But would you mind changing your name?"

Sheldon S. Cohen   Interview, 2000

SPREADING OUT

1955: Reflecting the growing importance of teen culture in American life, Paula Pascal and Fred Goldberg enjoy a Jewish high school fraternity dance.

Suburban developments like these homes in Kemp Mill Estates sprang up throughout the region.

The decades following World War II introduced enormous changes to Washington. As the federal bureaucracy expanded, newcomers flocked to the government boomtown. Over a third of Jewish workers in Washington were federal employees.

Returning veterans and newly arrived government workers contributed to the transformation of Washington from capital city into metropolitan region. Seeking new homes, they joined an exodus to the Maryland and Virginia suburbs. By 1956, half of the area's 81,000 Jews lived outside the city limits. Synagogues and many businesses followed.

At the same time, many local Jews joined the political and social movements of the 1950s and 1960s.

STERN *Office Furniture, Inc.*

Local Jewish-owned businesses thrived as the economy expanded.

Sam and Saul Stern of Stern Office Furniture

—Washington Star Photographer Robert Greiser

Offices Are More Than Furniture

1966: Brothers Sam (left) and Saul Stern transformed an 1880s building at 734 7th Street, N.W., into a modern showcase for their office furnishings business.

MOM & POP NO MORE

1951: The opening day brochure for Kann's new store in Arlington emphasized the full selection of fine fashions newly available in a suburban setting.

Kann's Virginia

WELCOMES YOU TO A NEW ADVENTURE

IN SHOPPING CONVENIENCE

A new Adventure ...in accessibility

The map-diagram reproduced below shows very clearly how you may reach Kann's Virginia easily and quickly, by your own, or public transportation.

W. V. & M. buses go directly past store, or into Clarendon Circle. If you are driving, you will find roads leading to Kann's Virginia are smooth and direct.

Kann's Virginia NORTH FAIRFAX DRIVE, NORTH WASHINGTON BOULEVARD, NORTH MONROE STREET and NORTH KIRKWOOD ROAD in ARLINGTON COUNTY, VIRGINIA

Many businesses moved to the suburbs to follow their customers. Corner groceries, pharmacies, and hardware stores became regional chains.

Stores remaining downtown faced new challenges. In 1968, riots erupted in Washington following the assassination of the Reverend Martin Luther King, Jr. Many Jewish-owned businesses along 7th Street, N.W., 14th Street, N.W., and H Street, N.E., were destroyed. Despite efforts by the Jewish Community Council and other agencies to assist the storeowners, most shuttered their doors permanently.

A downtown fixture since 1942, G Street Remnant Shop at 805 G Street, N.W., filled every floor of its seven-story building. In 1983, owner Judah Greenzaid moved the store to Rockville Pike in Maryland, promising his customers convenience, free parking, and proximity to the Beltway. The store's new name, G Street Fabrics, maintained the link to its downtown origins.

805 G Street N.W.

1950s: Irving and Kenneth Herman and brother-in-law Samuel Levin expanded Herman's Cut-Rate Market and created the grocery chain Jumbo Foods. Irving Herman is shown here (second from left) in the River Terrace store at 3439 Benning Road, N.E. In 1979, they opened Shoppers Food Warehouse, a no-frills grocery chain.

1960: Milton Elsberg opened a pharmacy in Arlington with Robert Gerber in 1938. By the late 1970s, Drug Fair had expanded into a regional chain of 176 stores. Many suburban stores stayed open all night—a marketing first.

1950s: Giant Food had grown into a regional chain with more than 50 stores in the city and suburbs, including this new store in Bethesda (above). Giant remained a locally owned family business until 1998 when it was sold to Royal Ahold, Inc. Seen above right are company founders Samuel Lehrman (left) and Nehemiah Cohen (right).

1957: Sidney Hechinger expanded his original wrecking business and lumberyard into a regional hardware chain catering to "do-it-yourself" homeowners. The Rockville store seen here opened on Memorial Day in 1957. Following Hechinger's death in 1958, his son John and son-in-law Richard England ran the family business.

1961: Company president John Hechinger (second from left) attends the ribbon-cutting of the Alexandria store, accompanied by his mother, Sylvia, manager Leroy Bendheim (center), and Hechinger chairman Richard England (right).

1963: Marilyn and Louis Glickfield opened their first major furniture store, shown here at 7th and I Streets, N.W. They combined their first names and called the new store Marlo's Furniture.

1972: Marlo's entered the suburbs with this 175,000-square foot furniture warehouse-showroom in Forestville, Maryland.

1951: The Coordinating Committee for the Enforcement of the D.C. Anti-Discrimination Laws, led by Mary Church Terrell and Jewish activist, Annie Stein, targeted several stores on 7th Street, N.W., during the fight for desegregation. After the group picketed in front of Hecht's for several months, the department store began serving black customers at its lunch counter in 1952.

FAIR-MINDED *Americans*

stay out of Hecht's

help end segregation at Hecht's lunch counter

"...'I have visited the capitals of many countries, but only in the capital of my own country have I been subjected to this indignity."

Hecht's violates the law
D.C. Restaurants must serve all well-behaved persons without discrimination - Law of 1873

Hecht's violates fair business practice
Millions of dollars are spent each year by Negroes at Hecht's - yet Negro Americans may not eat at the lunch counter

Hecht's violates democratic principles
Hecht's preaches brotherhood in full page ads, yet Hecht's practices segregation at its lunch counter

shop at these 7th st. stores that serve all
KANN'S
GOLDENBERG'S
KRESGE'S
WOOLWORTH'S
GRAND'S
MCCRORY'S

Coordinating Committee for the Enforcement of the D.C.
Anti-Discrimination Laws: 1103 Trenton Place S.E.

1980s: Morton's discount department store at 7th and D Streets, N.W., had employed black women as sales clerks since the 1930s. By the 1940s, owner Mortimer Lebowitz desegregated the store's dressing and rest rooms, years ahead of other downtown businesses.

Although Morton's stores on 14th Street, N.W. and H Street, N.E., were looted and burned during the 1968 riots, Lebowitz remained committed to his downtown stores. As the once thriving retail core declined, he was forced to close his stores in the 1980s.

Lebowitz (above center) is shown here with long-time employees Patricia Carr and Sam Braun.

1953: By its 50th anniversary, Pasternak's had grown from a small tailor shop to a four-story dress store on Connecticut Avenue, well-known for outfitting several First Ladies. The family sold the store in 1961 after 58 years in business.

1950s: In the city and the suburbs, Jewish-owned auto dealers catered to the new car-hungry culture. Harry Rosenthal (left) and son Bob (right) are seen here breaking ground for Rosenthal Chevrolet at the intersection of Glebe Road and Columbia Pike in Arlington in 1954.

WASHINGTON'S SEPHARDIC COMMUNITY

Jews from Morocco, Greece, Turkey, Iran, Iraq, Syria, Lebanon, Egypt, Yemen, and Latin America strengthen Washington's Sephardic community. They celebrate holidays like *Mimouna,* sing prayers using Sephardic melodies, and prepare special foods like *dafina, chouchouka,* and almond cigars.

In 1914 a small group of Greek and Turkish Jews founded Yom Tov Congregation, the city's first Sephardic prayer and burial group. They were soon joined by newly arrived Syrian Jews. Rabbi Solomon Ereza, an early community leader, secured permission for the group to meet at Washington Hebrew Congregation and later at the Hebrew Home on Spring Road.

A second wave of Sephardic immigrants, mainly Moroccans, arrived in Washington following World War II. Marcel Cadeaux and Albert Emsellem trained many of them in the beauty business.

By the mid-1960s the Sephardic community formed Magen David Sephardic Congregation. They held services at Tifereth Israel and later at Ohr Kodesh Congregation until moving to Bethesda in the 1980s.

"Our home was like the Sephardic JSSA (Jewish Social Service Agency)... My mother and father counseled and helped get people started... our door was always open."
— Irene Kaplan, daughter of Albert Emsellem

1950s: Albert Emsellem, son of the Chief Rabbi of Fez, became the patriarch of the post-war Sephardic community in the 1950s. Emsellem helped many Moroccan Jews by sponsoring them as students in his beauty school – The Capitol Beauty Institute – at 1012 H Street, N.W. Emsellem and his wife, Stella, are shown above at their first shop in Washington, Louey Venn of London, Inc., at 1224 Connecticut Avenue, N.W.

1998: Member Annie Totah designed the new 450-seat Magen David Sephardic Congregation Beit Eliahu Synagogue in Rockville, Maryland.

REAL ESTATE BOOM

Jewish builders and real estate developers played a major role in downtown and in the suburbs during Washington's postwar building boom.

As wartime restrictions ended, builders rushed to meet the pent-up housing demand with new construction in the city's outer neighborhoods and suburbs. The G.I. Bill provided veterans with low interest rates and made home ownership a reality for many. Several government agencies opened new offices outside the city, while federally supported highway and bridge projects encouraged the growth of new residential and commercial districts.

Many Jewish builders and real estate developers were recent immigrants who entered the business on a small scale, constructing or investing in modest projects while maintaining a small store. Some firms became family affairs, as sons and daughters expanded from building to selling and managing large properties including apartment complexes, office buildings, and suburban malls and subdivisions.

1938: Albert Small left his father's 7th Street, N.W., hardware store to sell commercial properties for the Cafritz Company before opening his own business in the 1930s. Built in 1938, the Silver Spring Shopping Center at Georgia Avenue and Colesville Road, shown here, was one of his earliest projects and the first drive-in shopping center in suburban Washington.

Indian Spring Country Club

COLESVILLE PIKE AND FOUR CORNERS
SILVER SPRING, MARYLAND

INDIAN SPRING COUNTRY CLUB WENDERINGS

(SECOND SPASM OF 1954 — SUMMER EDITION — ALBEIT A BIT LATE)

By Harry S. Wood

AT LONG LAST! NOW ...
revealed. We've been waiting ...
Board of Governors at its last ...
the REAL FACTS EXCLUSIV ...
we anticipated, with conseque ...

KAYWOOD GARDENS APARTMENTS
OFFICE: 4101 KAYWOOD PLACE
MT. RAINIER, MD.

RENTAL NOTICE
RENT PAYABLE AT OFFICE IN ADVANCE

1930s-1950s: Russian immigrant Abraham Kay got his start as a grocer on North Capitol Street in the 1920s and began building apartment houses while still running his store. In 1936, he formed Kay Construction Company and built in the Maryland suburbs. Early projects included Kaywood Gardens in Mt. Rainier.

In 1939, Kay purchased the Indian Spring Golf and Country Club at Four Corners in Silver Spring. He built 300 new homes on the golf course, extending club membership to new homeowners. After Beltway construction threatened the club's golf course, Kay moved Indian Spring to an expanded new facility in Glenmont in 1954.

1950s: Abraham Kay's son Jack entered the construction business at age 21. He built hundreds of suburban homes and apartment projects in Montgomery and Prince George's counties, such as this housing development in Kemp Mill Estates. He later started Kay Management Company.

Typical of Kay Construction Company's carefully planned land development ideas are these street scenes from Kemp Mill Estates. Notice how the natural contour of the land has been retained.

AMERICANA APARTMENT COMMUNITIES
CARL M. FREEMAN MANAGEMENT

CARL M. FREEMAN'S
AMERICANA Hampshire APARTMENTS

1950s: Carl Freeman responded to the postwar housing shortage by building thousands of contemporary ramblers and garden apartments in Washington and Maryland. Shown here is an advertisement for his garden-style Americana apartments in Silver Spring.

1968: Bernard and Carl Gewirz, sons of local developer and philanthropist Morris Gewirz, partnered with Albert H. Small, Robert Smith, Robert Kogod, and Edward Kaplan to develop several buildings along the K Street corridor. Seen below is the Montgomery Building at 1776 K Street, that they developed in 1968.

WEIHE BLACK KERR & JEFFRIES ARCHITECTS

1959: Lithuanian-born Morris Cafritz arrived in Washington in 1898. After owning several businesses including bowling alleys, Cafritz built houses and apartments throughout the city in the 1920s. He became known as "Mr. Office Building" when he began developing boxy 12-story office buildings along K Street, N.W. His Universal South building at 1825 Connecticut Avenue is shown here.

Salesman Morton Luchs and construction foreman Herbert Shannon opened their full-service real estate office in 1906 and developed neighborhoods like Burleith and Rollingwood. By the 1980s the family-owned firm was one of the area's largest. Services included insurance, commercial and residential leasing, sales, and property management. The company's early office (above) was at 704 13th Street, NW.

2000: Albert Small's son, Albert H. Small, founded Southern Engineering with Hermen Greenberg in 1950 and built more than 20,000 homes, condominiums, and office buildings throughout the region.

Shown below is Somerset House in Chevy Chase, Maryland built in partnership with Greenberg, Morton Funger, and Ralph Ochsman.

1965: Samuel Eig arrived in Washington in 1916 from Russia and soon began building homes in Takoma Park and Northwest Washington. Shown above is the Washingtonian Towers Apartment building next to Interstate 270 in Gaithersburg. When Interstate 370 in Gaithersburg opened in 1990, it was named the Sam Eig Highway.

1960s: Russian immigrant Charles E. Smith moved from New York to Washington in 1942 and began building apartment houses. By 1960, his son Robert Smith and son-in-law Robert Kogod had joined the family firm. In the 1960s, the Charles E. Smith Company built Crystal City in Arlington, a complex of offices, apartments, and hotels connected by underground shopping and entertainment.

August 17, 1964: The opening of the Capital Beltway stimulated suburban growth by making new homes more accessible to downtown workers.

NEW SYNAGOGUES

Within Washington's city limits and beyond, old and new synagogues flourished.

Jewish congregations moved north and west away from the city's core, constructing modern new synagogues with expanded schools, social rooms, and kitchens. New congregations formed on the outskirts of the city and in surrounding neighborhoods in Montgomery County and Northern Virginia.

"A good man leaveth an inheritance to his children's children" Proverbs 13

MONTGOMERY COUNTY JEWISH COMMUNITY, INC.
CHEVY CHASE, MARYLAND

1947: Young Jewish families in Chevy Chase and Silver Spring organized Montgomery County Jewish Community (MCJC). By 1952 the synagogue-center had engaged a fulltime rabbi and later built a synagogue on land donated by real estate developer Sam Eig. MCJC changed its name to Ohr Kodesh Congregation in 1966.

"I was waiting with my wife for a bus outside a shoe store on Wilson Boulevard. We heard singing and we looked at each other and I said, 'I'm sure that's Hebrew.' And sure enough over the shoe store was a synagogue! So we joined right away."

— Jerome Dick Interview, 2004

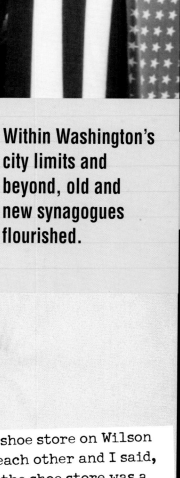

1959: Ohev Sholom, at 5th and I Streets, N.W., merged with Congregation Talmud Torah in 1958. In 1960, the combined Ohev Sholom Talmud Torah built a new synagogue on upper 16th Street, N.W. In 1959, Talmud Torah's original building on E Street, S.W., was demolished as part of an urban renewal project.

1960s: In 1964, residents of the newly redeveloped Southwest founded a Reform congregation, Southwest Hebrew Congregation. Renamed Temple Micah in 1968, the congregation shared space with St. Augustine's Episcopal Church at 600 M Street, S.W. Temple Micah added a menorah on the rooftop alongside the church's cross.

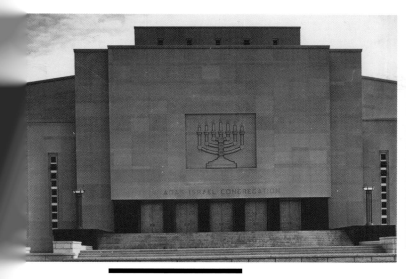

1951: Adas Israel dedicated its new synagogue at Connecticut and Porter Streets, N.W.

1956: When Temple Sinai dedicated its new Military Road synagogue, a 2000-year old stone from the Third Wall of Jerusalem was used as the cornerstone. Seen from left to right at the cornerstone laying are congregation president David Yentis, Rabbi A. Balfour Brickner, and United Nations Delegate Paul G. Hoffman.

1955: President Dwight D. Eisenhower spoke at the dedication of Washington Hebrew's new building at Massachusetts Avenue and Macomb Street, N.W.

CONGREGATION SHAARE TIKVAH

1965: Congregation Shaare Tikvah consecrated ground in Temple Hills, Maryland, for a new synagogue. The congregation was formed by a merger of three small synagogues created in the 1940s by federal workers living in southeast Washington: B'nai Jacob, Beth Israel, and the Washington Highlands Jewish Center.

THE JEWISH STAR

BI-WEEKLY DEVOTED TO JEWISH AND COMMUNAL AFFAIRS FOR GREATER WASHINGTON, MARYLAND AND VIRG

TIFERETH ISRAEL

SHOMRAI EMUNAH

AGUDAS ACHIM

BETH SHOLOM

BETH EL TEMPLE

INAUGURAL EDITION

FIVE NEW SYNAGOGUES OPENED THIS FALL   See page 14

NATION'S LEADERS WELCOME NEW JEWISH STAR   See page 16

| Plays and Players | Communal Life | Religious Services |
| Books | Radio-TV | Music |

1957: Tifereth Israel Congregation moved from Columbia Heights to Shepherd Park along upper 16th Street. Despite the decrease in the Jewish population in the area in the 1960s, congregants remained committed to their city location.

Shomrei Emunah, formed in 1952 by a handful of government workers, dedicated a small building on Eastern Avenue, N.E.

Beth Sholom built the area's largest Orthodox synagogue at 13th Street and Eastern Avenue, N.W.

With more than 6,000 Jews living in Northern Virginia by the mid-1950s, the two oldest congregations, Beth El Hebrew and Agudas Achim, built new, larger synagogues in Alexandria.

EXPANDING IN ALL DIRECTIONS

Local organizations joined the migration as the center of Jewish life shifted from city to suburbs. Jewish communal institutions expanded to support the growing population.

By the 1950s, historic downtown facilities were aging and inadequate to meet the needs of the expanding regional community. Real estate developer Charles E. Smith led the effort to move the Jewish Community Center, Hebrew Home for the Aged, and the Jewish Social Service Agency to a unified location in Montgomery County. In 1969, the three organizations opened new buildings on a 21-acre site on Montrose Road in Rockville. By the 1980s the United Jewish Appeal (UJA) moved to the same site, followed by the Jewish Community Council in the 1990s, creating a centralized campus of Jewish institutional life.

For many years the UJA, founded in Washington in 1937, had led fundraising campaigns in support of Jewish settlement in Palestine. By the 1960s, the UJA increased support for local Jewish organizations as well.

1959: Miriam Bazelon served as the first woman president of the Jewish Social Service Agency. By the mid-1960s, JSSA had evolved, in Bazelon's words, from giving "breadbaskets to the poor" to become a major provider of a broad range of professional social services.

1964: By the 1960s, UJA began to take on a greater role in fundraising for local programs. Here with local philanthropist Paul Himmelfarb (center) are local UJA leaders, from left to right, Dr. Seymour Alpert, Rabbi Isadore Breslau, Joseph Ottenstein, and UJA President Hymen Goldman.

UNITED JEWISH APPEAL
of Greater Washington

1959

Honor Roll of Contributors

REGULAR AND SPECIAL FUND

To build new homes, new lives, new hope in Israel, the U.S. and lands overseas

1 OUT OF 3 *STILL* NEEDS YOUR HELP

1959: UJA's annual fundraising campaigns were conducted by community volunteers in person-to-person solicitations. The Honor Roll, published each year, listed each Washington supporter who contributed ten dollars or more.

HEAR THE NEED.

GIVE THE ANSWER.

Super Sunday
Counting On...Counting Plan.

652-6480   JANUARY 17

UJA FEDERATION OF GREATER WASHINGTON
6935 ARLINGTON RD. BETHESDA MD 20814-5268

1976: UJA expanded its role to become the United Jewish Appeal Federation of Greater Washington, acting as the centralized fundraising body for local Jewish agencies and Israel. In 1978, the Federation initiated its "Super Sunday" phone-a-thon, engaging hundreds of volunteers in an annual fundraising event.

UNITED JEWISH APPEAL 1965

Your UJA Gift means Life, Hope, Freedom all over the world

1965: The Government Division became one of the most active fundraising divisions within UJA. Federal workers in the Post Office, IRS, Patent Office, and other agencies volunteered to solicit their fellow Jewish workers for support.

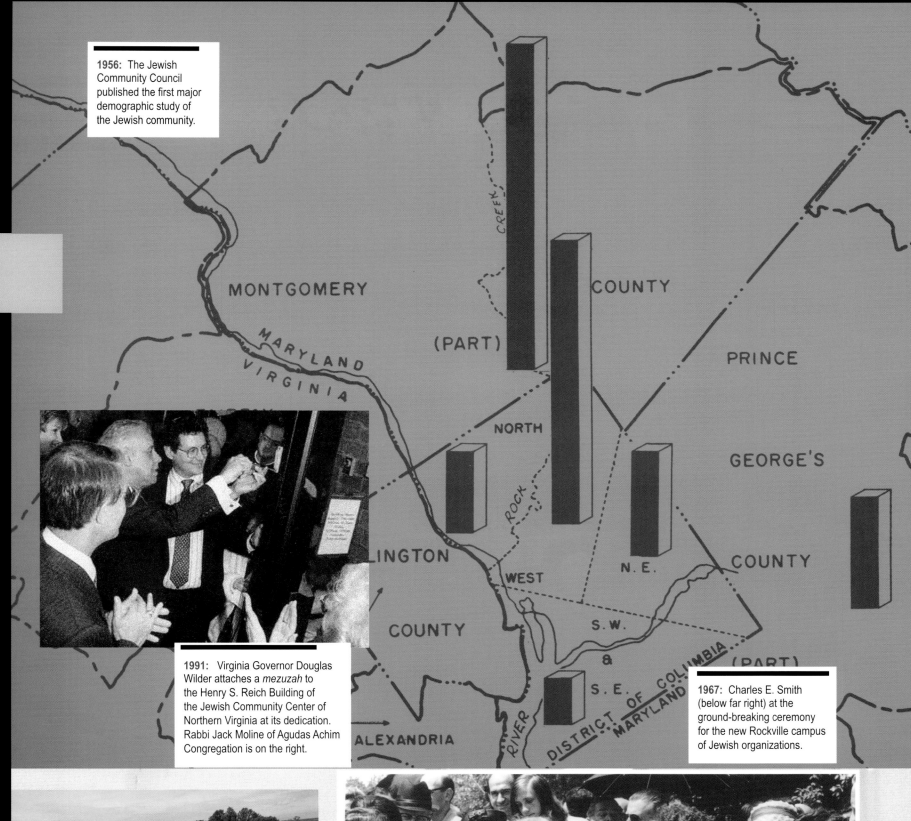

1956: The Jewish Community Council published the first major demographic study of the Jewish community.

1991: Virginia Governor Douglas Wilder attaches a *mezuzah* to the Henry S. Reich Building of the Jewish Community Center of Northern Virginia at its dedication. Rabbi Jack Moline of Agudas Achim Congregation is on the right.

1967: Charles E. Smith (below far right) at the ground-breaking ceremony for the new Rockville campus of Jewish organizations.

1990: After 5,000 people attended a "Hanukah Happening" in Northern Virginia in 1977, the Jewish Community Center of Northern Virginia (JCCNV) formed. Located in a former school on Little River Turnpike in Fairfax, the JCCNV offered classes, programs, and recreational activities for the growing Northern Virginia Jewish population. In 1990, the JCCNV dedicated a new building on the same site, shown here under construction.

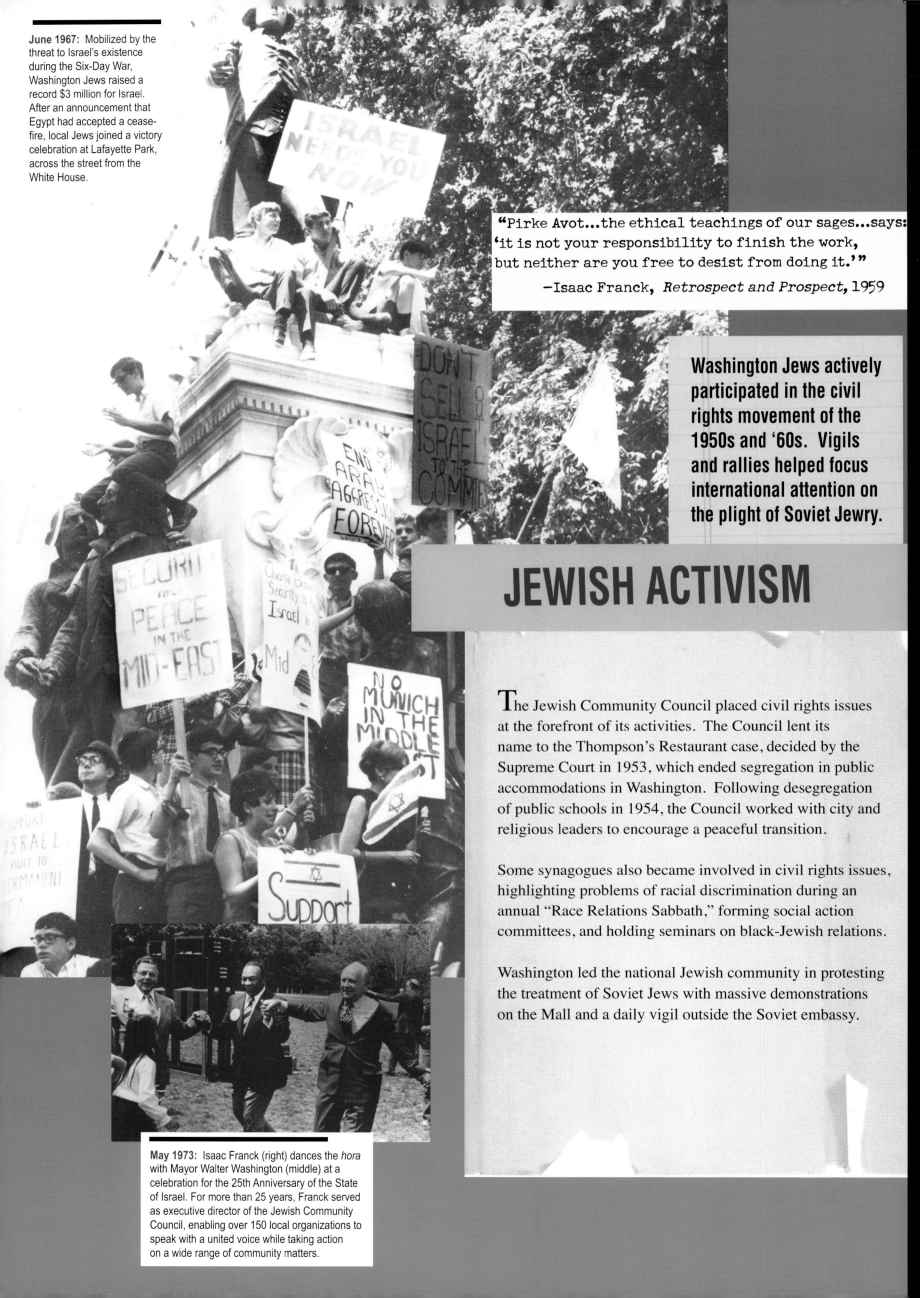

June 1967: Mobilized by the threat to Israel's existence during the Six-Day War, Washington Jews raised a record $3 million for Israel. After an announcement that Egypt had accepted a cease-fire, local Jews joined a victory celebration at Lafayette Park, across the street from the White House.

ISRAEL NEEDS YOU NOW

DON'T SELL ISRAEL TO THE COMMIE

END ARAB AGGRESSION FOREVER

SECURITY AND PEACE IN THE MID-EAST

NO MUNICH IN THE MIDDLE EAST

SUPPORT ISRAEL RIGHT TO PERMANENT

Support

"Pirke Avot...the ethical teachings of our sages...says: 'it is not your responsibility to finish the work, but neither are you free to desist from doing it.'"

—Isaac Franck, *Retrospect and Prospect,* 1959

Washington Jews actively participated in the civil rights movement of the 1950s and '60s. Vigils and rallies helped focus international attention on the plight of Soviet Jewry.

JEWISH ACTIVISM

The Jewish Community Council placed civil rights issues at the forefront of its activities. The Council lent its name to the Thompson's Restaurant case, decided by the Supreme Court in 1953, which ended segregation in public accommodations in Washington. Following desegregation of public schools in 1954, the Council worked with city and religious leaders to encourage a peaceful transition.

Some synagogues also became involved in civil rights issues, highlighting problems of racial discrimination during an annual "Race Relations Sabbath," forming social action committees, and holding seminars on black-Jewish relations.

Washington led the national Jewish community in protesting the treatment of Soviet Jews with massive demonstrations on the Mall and a daily vigil outside the Soviet embassy.

May 1973: Isaac Franck (right) dances the *hora* with Mayor Walter Washington (middle) at a celebration for the 25th Anniversary of the State of Israel. For more than 25 years, Franck served as executive director of the Jewish Community Council, enabling over 150 local organizations to speak with a united voice while taking action on a wide range of community matters.

Student Vigil for Civil Rights

1958: Civil rights activist Marvin Caplan helped found Neighbors Inc., a community group that encouraged white residents to remain in integrated neighborhoods such as Manor Park, Brightwood, Shepherd Park, and Takoma.

1964: Jewish, Catholic, and Protestant theological students from across the country organized a 24-hour vigil at the Lincoln Memorial to urge the Senate to pass the Civil Rights Act. Local synagogue sisterhoods provided kosher food to the Jewish students. Students kept vigil in three-hour shifts for 65 days until the bill was passed on June 19, 1964.

1958: Beth El Hebrew Congregation's Rabbi Emmet Frank spoke out against Virginia's policy of "massive resistance" to school integration. In his Yom Kippur sermon, he denounced "vocal segregationists… who have placed in jeopardy our nation" and reminded congregants that "the Jew cannot remain silent to injustice." Editorial attacks and bomb threats followed. Rabbi Frank is seen here with policemen checking his car after a bomb threat.

1960: Civil rights leaders Roy Wilkins (left) and A. Philip Randolph (second from the left) joined Hyman Bookbinder on a picket line outside Glen Echo amusement park. Bookbinder, then an AFL-CIO lobbyist, joined with other Jewish neighbors and Howard University students in protesting the whites-only policy of the popular suburban Maryland park. After a summer of protests, the park quietly desegregated when it re-opened the next spring.

1970-1991: Protesting on behalf of Soviet Jews denied permission to emigrate from the Soviet Union, Washington Jews maintained a daily noontime vigil outside the Soviet Embassy on 16th Street, N.W., for more than 20 years. Local synagogues and Jewish organizations were assigned specific days to help ensure daily attendance. The vigil ended in 1991, as Soviet policies changed and thousands of Jews were permitted to emigrate.

1987: On the eve of the Reagan-Gorbachev summit meeting in Washington, D.C., 250,000 people participated in a rally for Soviet Jewry on the Mall. The Jewish Community Council coordinated attendance of 50,000 Washington-area Jews.

1971: Protesters staged an all-night vigil at the Lincoln Memorial, beginning on the eighth and final day of Passover, to protest the treatment of Soviet Jews.

MARCHING FOR JOBS AND FREEDOM

During the 1963 March on Washington for Jobs and Freedom, the Jewish community took on several roles. Some marched, others provided marchers with food or shelter. Congregations opened their doors to hundreds of student marchers, sleeping bags in tow.

Isaac Franck, executive director of the Jewish Community Council of Greater Washington, (seen below, right) convened a meeting of local leaders with the Reverend Martin Luther King, Jr. prior to the March.

1961: Since 1956, the annual Ambassador's Ball has raised funds for Israel Bonds in honor of the anniversary of the State of Israel. Shown here at the 13th anniversary "Bar Mitzvah" Ball are event chairman Dr. Seymour Alpert and his wife, Cecile (back right) alongside Israeli Ambassador Avraham and Zena Harman. They are greeting Morris and Jennie Pollin.

THE NATIONAL AND INTERNATIONAL ARENA

Washington's confluence of religious, civic, and political life and its status as an international capital have made it a fitting backdrop for the national Jewish dialogue.

National Jewish organizations have long recognized the importance of Washington in the American Jewish political and cultural landscape. Lobbyists, activists, dignitaries, and philanthropists convene in Washington to discuss support for Israel and legislative issues of concern to the American Jewish community.

Israeli Embassy officials have made their mark on the local Jewish community, too. They join local synagogues, send their children to Jewish day schools, and volunteer on behalf of the community.

1969: Yitzhak Rabin, Israeli Ambassador to the U.S. from 1968-73, was the best-known Israeli official to reside in Washington. Rabin is shown here arriving at Adas Israel Congregation for the bar mitzvah of Gideon Argov, son of an Israeli Embassy official. In front, from left to right, are: Rabbi Stanley Rabinowitz, Ambassador Rabin, Prime Minister Golda Meir, and Simcha Dinitz, later Israel's Ambassador to the United States.

1971: Rabin and his wife, Leah, became ambassadors of Israeli culture as well as politics, promoting Israeli artists and musicians and attending local Jewish functions. When the Israel Philharmonic premiered at the Kennedy Center, these American Friends of the Israel Philharmonic were treated to a reception at the Israeli Embassy. Shown here from left to right are Ambassador Yitzhak Rabin, Conductor Zubin Mehta, Norman Bernstein, and David Lloyd Kreeger.

1953: I.L. Kenen founded the American-Israel Public Affairs Committee (AIPAC). Kenen worked to strengthen support for Israel on Capitol Hill and began publishing the bi-weekly "Near East Report" containing legislative updates on events affecting the U.S.-Israel relationship. AIPAC grew in numbers and influence in the 1960s and 1970s, becoming a strong voice for Israel with thousands of members engaged in grassroots lobbying efforts.

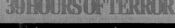

Above: Wesley Hymes (left) and other B'nai B'rith and B'nai B'rith Women employees are escorted to the Gramercy Inn by the Metropolitan Police.

Below: The ambassadors of Iran, Pakistan and Egypt leave the B'nai B'rith building after completing negotiations with Hanafi leaders.

NEAR EAST REPORT

SPECIAL SURVEY

Myths and Facts

Background to the Arab-Israel War

Jews in the Arab World

The Arab Boycott Today

A Supplement to the NEAR EAST REPORT · Aug. 1967 · 25 cents

1962: The Union of American Hebrew Congregations opened the Religious Action Center of Reform Judaism along Embassy Row to educate and mobilize American Jews on legislative issues and social concerns. Shown above are participants in the 1963 March on Washington.

1977: Washington's symbolic role as a center for national Jewish life was highlighted when a small group from the Hanafi Muslim sect took over the B'nai B'rith International headquarters at 17th and Rhode Island Avenues, N.W. For over 39 hours, 100 employees were held hostage. Hostages were also taken at the Islamic Center and D.C. City Council Chambers, where a reporter was killed.

After diplomats from Egypt, Iran, and Pakistan joined the police negotiations, the hostages were released. Following the incident, messages of support for B'nai B'rith poured in from around the world.

1969: President Lyndon B. Johnson appointed John Hechinger as the first Chairman of the D.C. City Council in 1967. Gilbert Hahn, appointed by President Richard M. Nixon, succeeded him as the second Council Chairman in 1969. Hahn served in that role until 1972, when the Home Rule Act took effect, providing for a locally elected mayor and city council. Here, outgoing Chairman Hechinger (left) greets incoming Chairman Hahn.

GOVERNMENT SERVICE

From Civil War-era postal clerks to ambassadors and presidential advisors, Jewish Washingtonians have served the community at local, national, and international levels.

President Lyndon B. Johnson received hate mail when he appointed Washingtonian Sheldon S. Cohen as Commissioner of the Internal Revenue Service in 1964. Thirty-seven years later, Senator Joseph Lieberman, an Orthodox Jew who did not campaign on the Sabbath, became the first Jewish candidate for Vice President.

Throughout the 1960s and 1970s, federal agencies once blocked to Jewish workers became increasingly open. The number of elected Jewish officials has steadily increased. Where once Jewish appointees were a matter of comment, they now serve without mention.

Washington Jews have also been involved in the city's governance since the 1886, when Adolphus Solomons was appointed to the Board of Education. Since then, members of the local Jewish community have helped shape civic life in the nation's capital as appointed and elected officials, fundraisers, and activists.

1961: President John F. Kennedy (far left) appointed Walter Tobriner as Chairman of the D.C. Board of Commissioners in 1961. Tobriner had earlier served as President of the Board of Education during the 1950s, when he oversaw the desegregation of the city's schools. Tobriner later served as U.S. Ambassador to Jamaica. Tobriner is shown here with President Kennedy presenting the keys of the city to Brazilian President João Goulart (center), in 1962.

1964: A founder of the "Voteless DC" League of Women Voters, Nettie Ottenberg spent a lifetime trying to bring about social change and voting rights for Washingtonians. Here, Ottenberg, seated in back left, encourages District voters to register and vote in the city's first local elections in over 150 years.

1977: Stuart Eizenstat (right) moved to Washington as a domestic policy advisor to President Jimmy Carter. He made the city his home when he served as president of the Jewish Community Center of Greater Washington from 1989 to 1991. Eizenstat held several positions in the Clinton administration, but claims his place in Jewish history as the architect of Holocaust-era restitution agreements.

1990: Partner in the real estate firm JBG Companies, Washingtonian Joseph B. Gildenhorn (left) served the community as president of the Hebrew Home and The Jewish Federation of Greater Washington. In 1988 he accompanied President George Bush to Israel, and the following year was appointed Ambassador to Switzerland.

Stuart Bernstein
Ambassador of the United States of America
to the Kingdom of Denmark

2001: Ambassador Stuart Bernstein grew up in Washington, attending Sunday School at the Jewish Community Center on 16th Street. President George W. Bush appointed Bernstein Ambassador to Denmark in 2001.

1994: Washingtonian and consumer advocate Ann Brown served as Chairman of the U.S. Consumer Product Safety Division from 1994 to 2001. Brown is shown here with Vice President Al Gore at her swearing-in ceremony.

1964: When Sheldon S. Cohen became IRS Commissioner, he was among the first Washington-born Jews to be appointed to the highest levels of government, and, at age 36, among the youngest. Commissioner Cohen (left) advises President Lyndon B. Johnson on national tax policy.

A diversity of school, synagogue, and camp programs reinforced Jewish identity.

GROWING UP JEWISH

Synagogue school programs expanded and new Jewish day schools opened in the postwar decades. Teenage social life revolved around Jewish fraternities, sororities, and Zionist youth groups during the 1950s and 1960s. Summer camps provided an opportunity for girls and boys to explore the great outdoors, make new friends, and learn Jewish values. Rituals like *bar* and *bat mitzvah* and confirmation marked Jewish milestones.

1960: Camper Janice Goldblum took this snapshot of nearby Fort Ritchie during her first summer at Camp Louise. For more than 80 years, Camps Airy and Louise in Maryland's Catoctin Mountains have combined swimming, hiking, and crafts with Jewish learning and Shabbat services for campers from the Baltimore and Washington D.C. area.

1940s: The Zionist youth group Habonim bought a 287-acre farm near Annapolis that became Camp Moshava, seen here (camper Leo Cohen in foreground). Jewish girls and boys learned skills like carpentry and camping, needed to live life on a *kibbutz* in Israel. As adults, most did not move to Israel for *kibbutz* life, but many retained strong ties to the Jewish state.

1960: Located on the Chesapeake Bay near Plum Point, Maryland, Kaufmann Camp served over 20,000 Jewish children from Washington between 1952 and 1984. Here, camp director Dr. Phil Fox leads campers in Friday evening services in the Recreation Hall.

1982: Gesher Jewish Day School opened as a kindergarten housed at Agudas Achim Congregation in Alexandria, Virginia. The school outgrew its space and in 1994 moved to the Jewish Community Center of Northern Virginia. Here, the kindergarten class participates in a Sabbath program with Rabbi Sheldon Elster and teacher Susan Koss.

1960s: First established in Reform congregations in the late 19th century, confirmation for 15- and 16-year-old Jewish boys and girls encourages the continuation of Jewish education past *bar* and *bat mitzvah* age. Here, Rabbi Tzvi Porath poses with a confirmation class at Ohr Kodesh Congregation in Chevy Chase.

ודולה מלאכה
שֶׁמְכַבֶּדֶת
אֶת בְּעָלֶיה

Great is work, for it honors the worker.

1985: Traditionally, Jewish boys have celebrated their coming of age by reading publicly from the Torah when they turn thirteen. In the mid-20th century, Reform and Conservative congregations began offering comparable ceremonies for girls. Stephanie Drazin, shown here with her mother Annette Drazin and grandmother, Elizabeth Gossin, became a *bat mitzvah* at Har Shalom Congregation in Potomac.

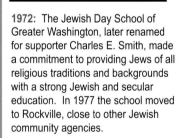

Cooperative
JEWISH CHILDREN'S SCHOOL
of Greater Washington

PEACE
MY LOVE OUR COUNTRY
FREEDOM   JUSTICE
BROTHERHOOD

Yearbook 1960-61

The Jewish Day School is a recipient agency of the United Jewish Appeal Federation

Mr. and Mrs. Herbert Stein

request the honour of your presence

at the Bar Mitzvah of their son

Jeremy Benjamin

on Saturday, the seventh of December

Nineteen hundred and fifty-seven

at nine o'clock in the morning

Montgomery County Jewish Community Center

2901 East West Highway

Chevy Chase, Maryland

1960: From 1947 to 1966, the Cooperative Jewish Children's School of Greater Washington appealed to parents who were not religiously observant. Classes focused on Jewish history and culture.

1972: The Jewish Day School of Greater Washington, later renamed for supporter Charles E. Smith, made a commitment to providing Jews of all religious traditions and backgrounds with a strong Jewish and secular education. In 1977 the school moved to Rockville, close to other Jewish community agencies.

1957: Formal engraved invitations, such as this 1957 invitation to Ben Stein's *bar mitzvah* at Montgomery County Jewish Community, invited friends and family to celebrate. Stein later became a speechwriter for President Nixon, an actor, and a game show host.

1977: Alan and Jeremy Bash, first-grade students at the Jewish Day School of Greater Washington and sons of Rabbi Marvin Bash of Arlington-Fairfax Jewish Congregation, practice blowing the *shofar* in preparation for the High Holidays.

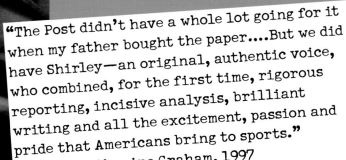

SHIRLEY POVICH (1905-1998) SPORTSWRITER EXTRAORDINAIRE

He called it a "joyride"—his journey from an Orthodox Jewish home in Bar Harbor, Maine, to his unparalleled 75-year-career at *The Washington Post*. He won every conceivable honor and was even elected to the Baseball Hall of Fame. But Shirley Povich was most proud of his Jewish heritage. He was a longtime member first of B'nai Israel and then of Adas Israel Congregation in Washington.

By 21, Povich was the youngest sports editor on any metropolitan newspaper. For decades, he was the most popular columnist at *The Washington Post*. He covered nearly every major sporting event of the 20th century, and he spent the last three decades of his life crusading to regain a baseball club for his city.

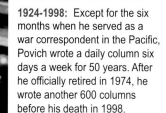

1924-1998: Except for the six months when he served as a war correspondent in the Pacific, Povich wrote a daily column six days a week for 50 years. After he officially retired in 1974, he wrote another 600 columns before his death in 1998.

1999: A successful businessman and lifelong fan of the Washington Redskins, Daniel Snyder, along with other family members and long-time investment partners, acquired the team in 1999. He was instrumental in making the team the most valuable sports franchise in the nation, as well as bringing legendary coach Joe Gibbs back to the Redskins' sidelines.

On sandlots and in gymnasiums across the country, Jewish children learned valuable lessons about teamwork, strength, and leadership.

PLAY BALL!

In the 1920s and 1930s, local Jewish children learned to play baseball, tennis, basketball and football at the Jewish Community Center, high schools, and neighborhood playgrounds. Local businesses sponsored teams like Southwest's Aztecs and Milton S. Kronheim, Sr.'s Bearcats, who played at 16th and Kennedy for 40 years.

Washington neighborhoods also turned out top-ranked Jewish boxers. From their childhood playgrounds, some Jewish Washingtonians went on to college and professional sports.

As Washington Jews rose to prominence in the community, the lure of owning a professional team attracted leading businessmen. Washington is the only city in the country in which Jewish families own three major sports franchises.

1913: The Young Men's Hebrew Association sponsored several sports teams, such as these baseball players in the city's athletic leagues.

2006: Head of Lerner Enterprises, the area's largest private real estate development company, Theodore N. Lerner, center, is the latest Jewish leader to acquire a professional sports team. The Washington Nationals brought baseball back to the District in 2005; the Lerners were granted ownership in May 2006. Three generations of Lerners, seen here at the stadium groundbreaking, are committed to building a winning tradition.

1964: Real estate developers Irene and Abe Pollin purchased the Baltimore Bullets in 1964 after being alerted to the sale by former NBA referee Arnold Heft. The team moved to the Washington area in the 1970s. The Pollins opened the Verizon Center, home to the renamed Wizards, in 1997, revitalizing the downtown area. Pollin, seated in the front row holding a basketball, is shown here with the Washington Wizards in 2005.

RECENT ENTRIES

Over 200 years have passed since Isaac Polock arrived in the new capital. Washington's Jewish community, now more than 200,000 people, is the sixth largest in the nation. Two centuries of entries in the community scrapbook tell stories of continuity and change, enduring tradition and adaptation to a changing city and an increasingly diverse community.

Today, Jewish Washingtonians continue to contribute — in voice and deed—to the evolving American Jewish experience.

Students arriving at the Charles E. Smith Jewish Day School. (background image)

Once centered downtown, the Jewish community is now concentrated in the suburbs and extends to the far reaches of the metropolitan area.

2004: Congregations Sha'are Shalom and Beth Chaverim in Loudoun County, Virginia extend the boundaries of Washington's Jewish community westward. In 2004, Sha'are Shalom consecrated a new temple, the first Jewish house of worship ever to be built in Loudoun County, in Leesburg. Seen here transporting the Torahs are congregants Harold Lurie, Howard Manas, and Rosalyn Lurie in a car driven by Janice Shankman.

1994: Founded in the Petworth neighborhood of Washington in the 1930s, Beth Sholom Congregation and Talmud Torah established a school and a chapel in Potomac in the 1970s. Encouraged by the ensuing move of many congregants, Beth Sholom continued to develop the suburban site. Renovations in the 1990s completed an expansive facility serving this modern Orthodox community.

2005: Six kosher restaurants served downtown Washington in the 1860s. Now, kosher groceries and eateries in the Maryland suburbs of Wheaton and Rockville serve the growing community. Here, patrons enjoy a Sunday night dinner at Max's Kosher Café on University Boulevard in Wheaton.

2003: Many Washingtonians serve a special role at the national site of Holocaust remembrance. Here, Nesse Godin of Silver Spring, Maryland, co-president of the local Jewish Holocaust survivors' organization, addresses a group from the U.S. Military Academy at West Point during their visit to the United States Holocaust Memorial Museum.

Washington JEWISH WEEK
2004 JCC MACCABI GAMES
August 2004

2004: The Jewish Community Center of Greater Washington hosted the annual JCC Maccabi Games. At this Olympic style event, over 1600 Jewish teen athletes from across the United States and seven other countries participated in sporting competitions including swimming, soccer, and tennis.

2005: Four hundred singers from more than 25 area synagogues commemorated the 350th anniversary of Jewish life in America at a concert at the Music Center at Strathmore in Bethesda, Maryland.

For many, community life still revolves around synagogues. Others forge ties through cultural, social, and political activities.

2000: New shops and restaurants have opened in these late 19th-century buildings along Seventh Street, N.W. across from the Verizon Center. Rudolph Behrend, who would become a Jewish civic leader and businessman, was born at 706 Seventh Street, N.W., in 1877. The building is now home to Legal Sea Foods.

BACK TO THE CITY

2002: Hillel: The Foundation for Jewish Campus Life moved its international headquarters into a new building on the corner of 8th and H Streets, N.W. Located in the heart of one of Washington's historic Jewish neighborhoods, Hillel stands adjacent to the former Washington Hebrew building.

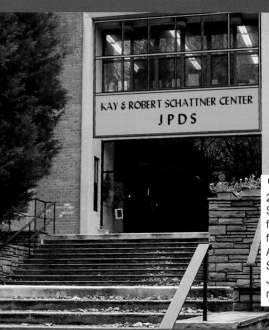

2002: The Jewish Primary Day School of the Nation's Capital found a new home in the former building of the Hebrew Academy at 16th and Fort Stevens Drive, N.W., returning Jewish learning to the site after more than twenty-five years.

A growing number of Jewish Washingtonians are returning to live and work in the city, participants in the revival of historic neighborhoods.

2004: Local developers are building hundreds of residences in revitalized downtown neighborhoods. JBG Companies, headed by Benjamin Jacobs, Donald Brown, and Joseph Gildenhorn, built Sovereign Square apartment building at 5th and Massachusetts Avenue, N.W., in 2004.

2004: Built by Adas Israel Congregation in 1908, this building was the home of Turner Memorial A.M.E. Church from 1951 until 2002. When the church moved to Hyattsville, three Jewish developers – Abe Pollin, Douglas Jemal, and Shelton Zuckerman – purchased the building and oversaw its restoration. Hundreds who had worshipped here for nearly a century – Jews and Christians alike – returned for the dedication of the Sixth and I Historic Synagogue.

1969: In 1968, construction of the Washington Metropolitan Area Transit Authority headquarters at 6th and G Streets, N.W., threatened the city's oldest synagogue building. The Jewish Historical Society of Greater Washington mobilized the community and saved the original 1876 Adas Israel synagogue with assistance from the local and federal governments. On a frigid December day, building engineers hoisted the more-than-270-ton synagogue onto a pair of dollies and moved the building three blocks east.

"This restoration is important to the culture of our people, because we have always considered the synagogue as the backbone of Jewish life. This first synagogue is a keepsake for all the people of Washington . . . ."

Albert Small   Interview, 1974

1974: Community contributions and a gift from Lillian and Albert Small, seen here at the rededication ceremony with Supreme Court Justice Arthur Goldberg, helped to restore the synagogue. Albert Small grew up two blocks away on 5th Street, N.W. His father, Isadore, worshipped in the building.

1970: The synagogue is shown here on its new foundation at 3rd and G Streets, N.W., shortly after the move. The building, maintained by the Jewish Historical Society of Greater Washington, is listed on the Washington D.C. Inventory of Historic Sites and the National Register of Historic Places.

A NEW HOME FOR AN OLD SYNAGOGUE

2003: At a Jewish Historical Society school program, first-graders from Kehila Chadasha Congregation in Maryland created these *tzedakah* boxes modeled after the historic synagogue.

In the city's first synagogue building, today's Washingtonians celebrate and learn.

1992: The Jewish Historical Society of Greater Washington maintains the historic synagogue as the Lillian and Albert Small Jewish Museum. The sanctuary is now used for educational programs and life cycle events, like this 1992 wedding of Richard Neugass and Margery Goldberg.

2005: Members of the Alperstein family have run businesses in the area for over a century. The first Alperstein's furniture opened in Baltimore in 1904. In 1933, Al Alperstein opened a furniture shop at 1020 Seventh Street, N.W. Across the street at 1015 Seventh Street, his nephew Richard continues the family business today.

While many family businesses have been sold, some Washingtonians continue businesses inherited from parents and grandparents.

Washington's Jews maintain close ties with Israel and add their voices to the debate about her present and future.

2003: On the 55th anniversary of the State of Israel, more than 100 Washingtonians joined 5,000 delegates from around the world at the General Assembly of the United Jewish Communities in Israel. Here, Washingtonians Susie Gelman (far left) and Michael Gelman (fourth from left), Co-Chairs of the General Assembly, lead a mile-long march through Jerusalem.

2002: American and Israeli teens gather at the Western Wall during an Ambassador for Tolerance trip to Israel. As part of the Jewish Experiences for Teens program sponsored by The Jewish Federation of Greater Washington and Partnership 2000, Washington teens learn about religious pluralism, tolerance and diversity with Israeli peers. Pictured here are Lawrence Burka, Andrea Waghelstein, Ben Friedmann, Josh Stanton, Ami Snyder, and Roniel Tessler.

Many local Jews embrace dynamic and inclusive expressions of Jewish tradition.

1998: When Amy Schwartzman became Senior Rabbi of Temple Rodef Shalom, a Reform congregation in Falls Church, Virginia, the congregation became the largest led by a woman rabbi. The Reform movement began ordaining women in 1972, followed by the Conservative movement in 1985.

1975: Founded in 1975 to embrace a diversity of sexual and gender identities, Bet Mishpachah Congregation now has several hundred members. Its Torah mantles are decorated with rainbows, a symbol of pride for the gay and lesbian community. They are inscribed with a verse from Genesis 9:13: "When I see the rainbow, I will remember My covenant."

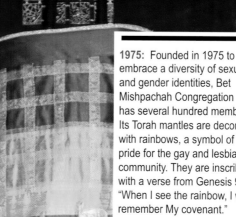

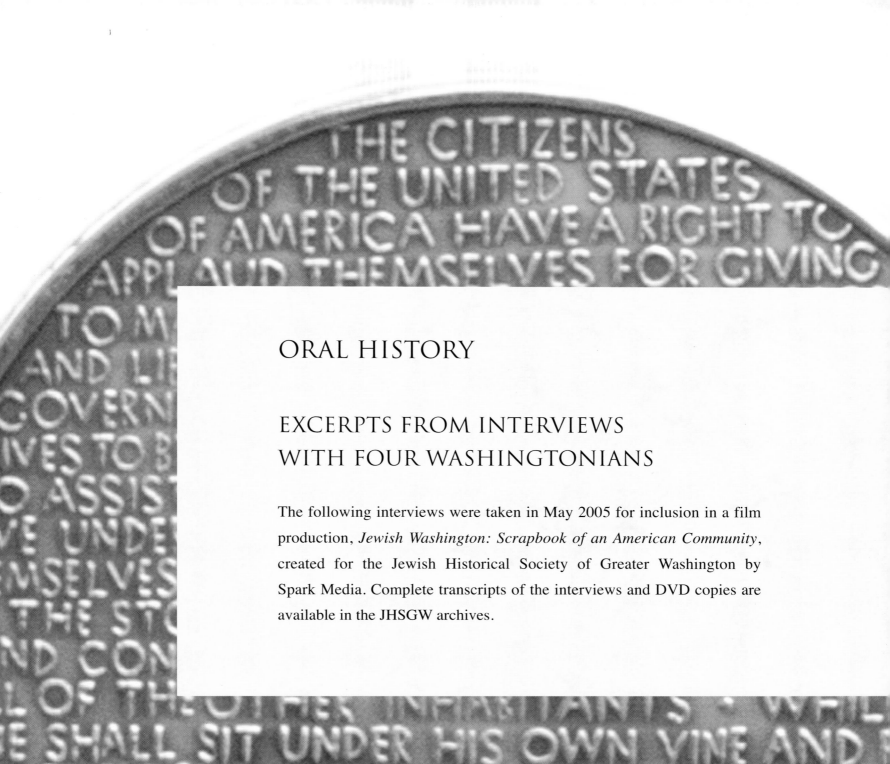

ORAL HISTORY

EXCERPTS FROM INTERVIEWS
WITH FOUR WASHINGTONIANS

The following interviews were taken in May 2005 for inclusion in a film production, *Jewish Washington: Scrapbook of an American Community*, created for the Jewish Historical Society of Greater Washington by Spark Media. Complete transcripts of the interviews and DVD copies are available in the JHSGW archives.

RUTH BADER GINSBURG
Associate Justice, United States Supreme Court

What brought me to this capital city was President Jimmy Carter, who decided he was going to change the face of the U.S. Judiciary. Quite literally, because when he became president, there was only one woman on a federal appellate bench in the entire nation . . . He was determined to change that. By the time he left office, and he had only one term, he had appointed eleven women to Courts of Appeals, and over twenty-five to federal trial courts. He set a pattern that no president abandoned.

We did not have a kosher home, but my mother lit candles every Friday night. My paternal grandparents were alive in my growing-up years. The entire family on my father's side gathered for *seders* and at Hanukkah, when the children collected Hanukkah *gelt*. I went to religious school. . . I was confirmed, but not *bat mitzvahed* because that ceremony did not exist at the time.

I would say my Jewishness…my heritage as a Jew, coming from the People of the Book, and from my parents, was to love learning. The other main theme is captured by the statement from Deuteronomy: *Tzedek, Tzedek, Tirdof* ('Justice, Justice, Thou Shalt Pursue') … I have portrayals of that message in lithographs, in glass sculpture, the words are all over my chambers. The notion, 'Justice, Justice, Thou Shalt Pursue,'…well, that is my work…to pursue justice. We have laws and many of them require interpretation because Congress is not always as clear as one might hope it…would be. A jurist has principles that guide her in interpreting text. One of them is that the law is designed to govern, should be designed to govern, a just and humane society.

When I was a new judge on the Court, the Court's wonderful clerk came to me and said, "Every year, we get requests from Orthodox Jews to amend the certificate of membership in the Court's Bar, because that certificate reads, just as every executive decree does, 'In the year of our Lord so and so….'" I thought that was an entirely reasonable request. But tradition plays a large part in the way courts work. The first thing I did, I checked what the other federal courts were doing. I was embarrassed to discover that the bar membership certificates for the court on which I served for thirteen years, the U.S. Court of Appeals for the D.C. Circuit, also read, 'In the year of our Lord.' Chief judges from the Court of Appeals readily agreed to change that practice. That was an easy endeavor, I barely had to ask and the change was made.

But here (at the Supreme Court) it was harder, because this place is very tradition-bound. I was told by a colleague, "Why are you making a fuss about this? It was good enough for Brandeis, it was good enough for Cardozo and Frankfurter." I said, "Stop. It's not good enough for Ginsburg." The certificate, years ago altered, now gives people an option.

May 27, 2005

FRANK RICH

Columnist, *The New York Times*

My father's family first resided in Washington before the Civil War. They were German-Jewish immigrants who came in and started a shoe store downtown that would ultimately blossom into a business that lasted from the late 1860s to the 1980s.

My mother's family were Russian-Jewish immigrants who settled in the Lower East Side of Manhattan, moved to Brooklyn and my mother, her sister and her parents moved to Washington after the stock market crash during the Depression. It was there that she met my father who really was from one of those old native Jewish Washington families.

I grew up in Washington as a stage-struck kid in a city that was a company town of government. One of my earliest memories . . . was watching the Kennedy inaugural parade. I absolutely think it has had an enormous influence on me to this day because my whole career has been about culture and politics and where they meet, and about culture and news and history and where they meet.

I do think that there's a Jewish element to it too, because even the small Jewish community that I grew up in had a cultural element that was often in those days more assertive than the general culture of pre-Kennedy Center Washington.... I vividly remember my mother as a young housewife in the 1950s going to the National Council of Jewish Women and taking oil painting classes that were taught by, they weren't famous then, but they were taught by Morris Louis and Kenneth Noland. There was always that kind of thing going on that made a difference.

One of the things I liked about Temple Sinai or the atmosphere there was that there was a sense of concern about culture and literature which was not really true in the public schools. . . I was *bar mitzvahed* . . . at Temple Sinai on Military Road before an ark designed by Boris Aronson, a Broadway set designer . . . who would go on to design *Fiddler on the Roof* and a bunch of others, all the Stephen Sondheim musicals. So there was this element of Washington that paid off for me in my development. It might not have been the same if I had been in New York from the get-go.

June 3, 2005

IRENE EMSELLEM KAPLAN

President, The Jewish Federation of Greater Washington

The Washington Jewish community is a very interesting community. It is a community that started mostly as transplants . . . What we found in our last demographic study is that more people are coming to Washington and staying than are coming in and doing their job, and then going back to where they came from . . . We are the only community on the East Coast that is actually growing. Our community is now 215,000 Jews.

My father was an immigrant to this country [from Morocco]. He came here in 1928 . . . and then he found a beauty shop that was for sale here in Washington and he bought it and opened a shop on Connecticut Avenue . . . [later] he opened a beauty school. From the beauty school, he started bringing more and more Sephardim into the area . . . they came in through the education permits my father was able to obtain for the school. He would bring them here and start them off in business.

Our home was like the Sephardic JSSA (Jewish Social Service Agency). Whenever anyone had a problem, it was "Call Uncle Albert." That was my father. That was how they referred to him. And my mother and father counseled, helped get people started, gave them the means to get started. Our door was always open for people who came and had no place to go. They would stay with us until they could get established.

I can't remember a time growing up where we didn't have someone in our home who needed a place before they set out in the world here in the United States . . . in one bedroom, we had four beds. You couldn't walk between them. It was wall to wall beds where people were sleeping. Because that's how they got started. It was this caring for each other. There was a concern for helping others. And you know, the real idea of *Tikkun Olam* — one person at a time.

What I picked up was a sense of community that is so much bigger than myself. And if everyone didn't help and if everyone didn't pitch in, than there was no community . . . you do the most you can, not the least you can. That's what was instilled in me by my parents, by my father and my mother, that you are there to help. And it doesn't matter what your needs are. If you have more than the next person and they need help, then you help.

May 27, 2005

ALBERT H. SMALL, JR.
Real Estate Developer

My family began here three generations ago. My grandfather was born in Washington and my father was born in Washington and I have a son born in Washington, so we represent four generations of Jews in Washington . . . My grandfather worked in his father's store, my great-grandfather who I never knew, worked in his store right down on 7th Street, and had a hardware store catering to the building trades . . . My grandfather put together many real estate deals as a broker, and provided mortgage financing for those deals.

My grandfather was primarily a commercial developer; my father is primarily an apartment and commercial developer. I focused on the pure residential homebuilding side, and I actually gravitated to Northern Virginia . . . People used to joke, "Sonny, you're going over to Virginia. There are no Jewish people over there. We don't even know where the bridge is to cross over the river to get there! How did you find that to begin with, let alone make a career out of that environment?"

And . . . what's been fascinating to see in Northern Virginia, which was very true when I started there twenty-five years ago, was the Jewish population was actually quite small. It has grown enormously during the years I've been there. We used to joke that if we built a hundred houses a year, we might sell to the one Jew who moved to Northern Virginia. Now 20, 30, 40% of our sales are to Jews moving to the area who are working in the high tech firms that have now been very prolific in Northern Virginia . . . I used to drive by to one project on a regular basis, and I saw a sign, "Coming Soon" for a synagogue. And I now go by there, and I see the signs, "We are now on our third addition to the building" . . . And now we're building out in Loudoun County, Virginia, and I'm seeing the same story unfold as you get further out, and here's a new sign, "Coming Soon."

June 2, 2005

AFTERWORD

Once upon a time I too kept a scrapbook. In it I pasted notes and cards, photos and mementos — a menu, a pressed flower, a ticket stub —meant to recall significant moments in my life. Alas, that scrapbook is long gone, thrown away in one of those frenzied moments of taking stock of one's possessions and clearing the clutter. Only long after it disappeared did I come, as an historian, to recognize the immense value of scrapbooks. The variety of images pasted onto their leaves convey a story of their authors' lives unmediated by time and the distance of fading memory. A newspaper article, clipped as it appeared, listing the careers open to women at the end of the nineteenth century tells us a great deal about the woman who decided to paste that in her scrapbook. A letter preserved welcoming a new student and warning her of what life would be like as one of only two women studying amidst a swarm of men becomes the material out of which the historian later writes history.

So too this scrapbook of Washington Jewry becomes our mnemonic device. Like so many others who found their way to Washington, D.C. from elsewhere, I claim the right of saying "our." Our scrapbook conveys the fabric of Jewish life as lived out in the federal city, in the nation's capital. Sometimes, that fabric is literal, as in the Behrend family circumcision gown; more often it is metaphorical as other objects, like an engraved cake knife, give heft to our memories.

Histories of the founding of American Jewish communities do exhibit striking similarities. Each community records, with pride, its first immigrants, its first cemetery, its first synagogue, its first public office holders. Each one is careful to list its particular web of agencies providing relief and foster care, education and social service, proving that the Jews of Columbus, Ohio, or Kansas City, Missouri, have fulfilled their historic obligation to care for their own, for the widowed and the orphaned. Thus our scrapbook has its pages devoted to our synagogues and communal institutions; and to how those who sustained them made a living. Washington's Jews started out as butchers, bakers, and grocers; and, long before they became real estate developers, physicians, and lawyers, they owned clothing stores and sold hardware.

But, even as so many pages of our scrapbook could find their way in between the covers of those of other American Jewish communities, our community is, indeed, truly distinctive. What stands out in our book is how many of its pages have been covered with mementos revealing our community's history to be deeply intertwined with the history of our nation's capital. As its population grew, so did ours. As they moved beyond the borders of the city, so did we. Our first synagogue was chartered by an act of Congress. A Jewish physician attended the mortally wounded Abraham Lincoln. Our nation's highest officers have joined us, as we dedicated a synagogue, laid a cornerstone, and celebrated 350 years of Jewish life in America. In turn our community has a long record of service to the federal city: at one time one-third of the Jews working in Washington were employed by its government. Others left their mark as elected federal officials and as their advisors and appointees. Even if they only sojourned here for a time, their history became our history, as they filled in blank pages in the scrapbook of what has become the sixth largest Jewish community in the United States.

Washingtonians everywhere are deeply indebted to the Jewish Historical Society of Greater Washington, and especially to its executive director Laura Cohen Apelbaum, for seizing the moment. Spurred by the 350th anniversary of American Jewish life, she recognized that the time had come to compile Washington Jewry's scrapbook. Its transformation from a museum exhibition into this striking album promises that, unlike the scrapbook of mine which disappeared so long ago, this one will remain to be read again and again, given to our children and grandchildren, and one day to become the pages out of which an historian in the future writes the history of the Jews of the nation's capital.

by Pamela S. Nadell, Ph.D.

Director of Jewish Studies Program, American University, Washington, D.C.

OBJECTS

The objects shown here were on display in the exhibition *Jewish Washington: Scrapbook of an American Community* at the National Building Museum.

American Jewish Tercentenary Medal, 1954.
This bronze medal (above) was minted to commemorate the 300th anniversary of Jewish life in the United States. Local interest in American Jewish history created by this commemoration led to the formation of the Jewish Historical Society of Greater Washington.
JHSGW Collections.

Celebrate 350 Medal, 2004.
Created for the 350th anniversary of Jewish life in the United States, this medal includes an excerpt from President George Washington's letter to the Hebrew Congregation in Newport, Rhode Island. In the 1790 letter, Washington described the United States government, "which to bigotry gives no sanction, to persecution no assistance…."
JHSGW Collections.
Gift of Mel Wachs.

Circumcision Gown, 1877.
Amnon and Sarah Behrend dressed their infant son, Rudolph, in this handmade gown for his *brit* (ritual circumcision).
JHSGW Collections.
Nordlinger-Behrend-Goldstein Family Archives. 2004.04

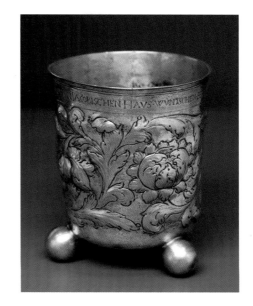

Wedding Cup, 1690.
This handmade silver wedding cup
is typical of the family heirlooms
brought by early Jewish immigrants to
Washington. The German inscription
around the top edge wishes the bridal
couple a long and happy life.

JHSGW Collections.
Gift of Edith Roth. 1992.01

Cake Knife and Plate, 1860s.
Adolphus Solomons and his wife
Rachel Seixas Phillips used these
housewares while entertaining in
their K Street, N.W., home.
The intertwined initials "A" "S"
are engraved on the knife handle.

Courtesy of B'nai B'rith
Klutznick National Jewish Museum.

**Yarmulke, Tefillin Bag, Tefillin,
1870s-1880s**
Leon Poppers used these ritual objects
while praying at Adas Israel's first
synagogue at 6th and G Streets, N.W.
An emigrant from Holland, Poppers
was an early and active member of
the congregation. Poppers' great-
grandson, Dr. Gerald Aurbach, became
a world renowned physician scientist
and maintained the family's link to the
Adas Israel Congregation.

JHSGW Collections.
Gift of Hannah Aurbach. 1999.51

District Grocery Store Sign, 1920s.

This sign hung over Harry's Market in Mt. Rainier, Maryland for seventy years. Leah and Harry Weinstein opened the store in 1924 and became original members of the District Grocery Store cooperative. Daughters Ruth and Vivien ran the store until 1995.

JHSGW Collections. Gift of Milton Weinstein. 1999.36

Pew from Washington Hebrew Congregation, 1898.

This is an original pew from the 8th and H Street, N.W. temple of Washington Hebrew Congregation.

JHSGW Collections. Gift of Brenda and Paul Pascal. 2002.18

Eternal Light from Washington Hebrew Congregation, 1898.

Washington Hebrew Congregation dedicated this *ner tamid* (eternal light) in memory of Henry King, Jr. King served as president of the congregation while the new temple was under construction.

JHSGW Collections. Gift of Robert Reich. 1975.01

Steamer Trunk, 1940.

Polish immigrants Fela and Siegfried Pollner escaped from Nazi Europe in February 1940. Sailing from Belgium to Argentina, they carried the family's belongs in this steamer trunk. Their son, Marco, arrived in the United States in 1947 and worked for the United Nations before moving to Washington.

JHSGW Collections. Gift of Marco Pollner. 1997.03

Shoemaker's Bench and Leather Punch, ca. 1920

In his shop at 1623 H Street, N.W., Nathan Ring, known as "shoemaker to the presidents," also repaired shoes for Supreme Court Justices and other government officials. His children remembered delivering brown paper packages of newly-shined shoes to the front door of the White House.

JHSGW Collections. Gift of Sandy Blank. 2003.26

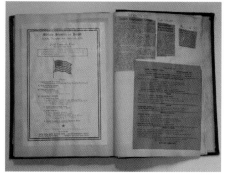

Jewish Community Center Scrapbook, 1942

The Jewish Community Center documented its wartime activities and cultural programs in annual scrapbooks such as this.

JHSGW Collections.
Gift of Jewish Community Center of Greater Washington. 2002.11

Jewish Lions Club Banner.

The Jewish Lions Club formed in 1937 as a social club for local teenage boys. As each club member left to serve in the armed services during World War II, a star with his name was embroidered on this club banner. All 25 club members who served eventually returned home safely.

Courtesy of Harry S. Kramer.

Ration Books and Victory Hair Pins, 1940s

With wartime shortages in effect, Washingtonians learned to save and re-use everything. Ration books, stamps, and tokens were used to purchase gas, rubber, nylon, butter, coffee, liquor, and sugar. Women were encouraged to "help Uncle Sam save steel" by re-using Victory Hair pins like these.

JHSGW Collections.
Gift of Edith and Charles Pascal. 1995.03

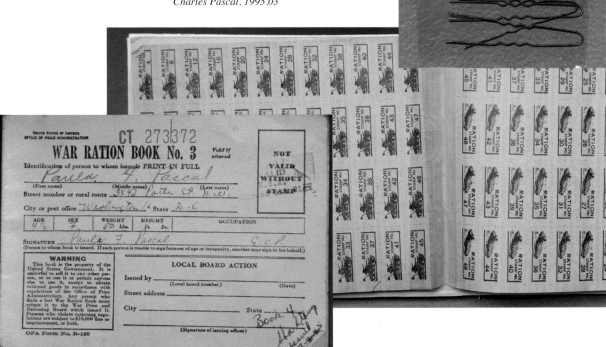

Menus
Hofberg's Deli Menu, 1940s
Hot Shoppes Menu, 1934

Hofberg's Deli at Georgia and Eastern
Avenues, N.W. and several area Hot
Shoppes were popular gathering places
for many Jewish teens.

Hofberg's menu: JHSGW Collections.
Gift of Ann Hofberg Richards. 1998.27

Hot Shoppes menu: JHSGW Collections.
Gift of Nadine Rubenstein. 1999.42

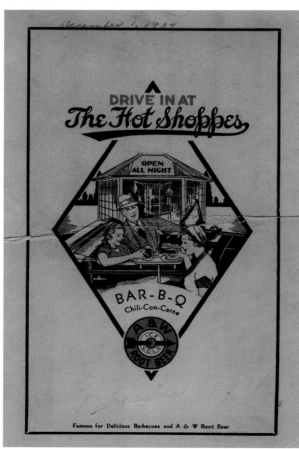

Bowl America Memorabilia
Amidst a surge in the national
popularity of bowling clubs and
leagues, Eddie Goldberg opened
the area's first major tenpin bowling
alley in 1958. Seen here at the
opening night of Shirley Tenpin
Bowl in Fairfax County, Virgnia, are,
from left to right, partners Samuel
Higger, Samuel Sobkov, Dr. Sollie
Katzman, and Eddie Goldberg.
Bowl America, as the chain became
known, included 25 bowling alleys
at its height.

Courtesy of Leslie Goldberg.

Typewriter
Famed sportswriter Shirley Povich composed many of his articles for *The Washington Post* on this typewriter.

Courtesy of B'nai B'rith Klutznick National Jewish Museum.

March on Washington Pennant, 1963
Hyman Bookbinder, lobbyist for the AFL-CIO and later the American Jewish Committee, carried this pennant in the 1963 March on Washington for Jobs and Freedom. Over 250,000 people attended the massive civil rights march and rally, which closed with the Reverend Martin Luther King, Jr.'s now famous "I Have a Dream" speech.

Courtesy of Hyman Bookbinder.

Buttons for Soviet Jewry, 1960s-1970s
Rabbi Aaron Pearlstein of Nevey Shalom Congregation in Bowie, Maryland, and his wife, Peggy, brought their young children to rallies for Soviet Jewry on the Mall, where they wore these buttons.

JHSGW Collections.
Gift of Peggy Pearlstein. 2004.22

Milton S. Kronheim, Sr.
For over 50 years, local liquor distributor Milton S. Kronheim, Sr. presided over a modestly appointed lunchroom at his northeast Washington warehouse. There he hosted presidents, lawmakers, Supreme Court Justices, sports figures, religious leaders, and businessmen.

Shown here in Kronheim's dining room around the late 1960s are, from left (sitting): Associate Justice William O. Douglas, Judge Simon Sobeloff, Milton S. Kronheim, Sr., Chief Justice Earl Warren, Associate Justice Thurgood S. Marshall. Standing from left are: Milton King, Judge David L. Bazelon, former Maryland Governor Theodore R. McKeldin, Stanley Rosenzweig, Judge J. Skelly Wright, Associate Justice William E. Brennan, Jr.

JHSGW Collections.
Gift of Milton S. Kronheim, Sr. Estate. 1998.54

Stained Glass Window

Housed in one of the oldest remaining commercial buildings in
Washington, Litwin's antique furniture store at 637 Indiana Avenue,
N.W., was one of the last remaining furniture stores that once
crowded the 7th Street neighborhood. Store owner Fred Litwin
purchased this stained glass window – originally from a Brooklyn
synagogue – in 1980. For over twenty years, until Litwin closed
his shop in 2003, the window hung in the back of his store.

JHSGW Collections.
Gift of Fred Litwin. 2003.6

600 I Street, N.W.:
One Building, Three Windows

An interactive display based on the
stained-glass window in the former Adas
Israel Synagogue at 6th and I Streets,
N.W. accompanied the exhibition at the
National Building Museum. Visitors
learned the history of the window and
then became "stained glass artists" by
creating their own design using colored
"window" pieces on a light box.

1908-1951

In 1908, Adas Israel
Congregation built a new
synagogue at 6th and I Streets,
NW. This photograph shows
the original stained-glass
window.

1951 – 2002

In 1951, Adas Israel moved
to a larger synagogue. Turner
Memorial African Methodist
Episcopal Church bought
the building and used it as
their church.

This is the new stained-glass
window that a church member
designed in the 1980s.

Today

In 2002, Turner Memorial
moved to Hyattsville, Maryland.
Three Jewish developers – Abe
Pollin, Shelton Zuckerman, and
Douglas Jemal – purchased the
building and made it a Jewish
space again.

Classic Glass of Alexandria,
Virginia, used old black and
white photographs to re-create
the window's original design.
They chose colors based on other
stained glass windows in the
sanctuary that dated back to
the building's construction.

VISITOR COMMENTS

Visitors to the exhibition at the National Building Museum were invited to share their own stories.

Share your memories and stories......

I grew up in N.W. Washington - my father came to work for the government in 1942 - I took dancing + acting at the JCC - went to Tifereth Israel on 14th & Euclid N.W. - went to Camp Louise - I bought baked goods at "The New Yorker Bakery" (their son is my husband) My parents were Gussie & Al Blankstein

Name _Marlene B. Fenster_
Address/Email
I feel part of this great exhibit.

Share your memories and stories......

My family came to Washington from Russia in the early 1900s. My great-grandfather had a tailor store on 1st St, NW, and his brother had his tailor store at 800 East Capitol St. My father's father came to DC from New York in the 1930s to find work. My father was born downtown. It's amazing to see so vividly and broadly the world (and city) they lived in. Thank you.

Name _Phil Margolies_
Address/Email

Share your memories and stories......

As a young French Jewish couple, recently settled in Washington, the success of American Jews shown in this exhibit has really moved us -
This warm feeling of a Jewish identity far transcends nationalities -

Share your memories and stories......

As a Russian Jew who recently immigrated to the US, I find this exhibit very uplifting! I wish there were more exhibits like this! Through this exhibit I rediscovered the Jewish history of the city that became so dear to me.

Name _Leonid Nikolayev_
Address/Email

Share your memories and stories......

I AM A NATIVE WASHINGTONIAN GROWING UP LIVING UPSTAIRS FROM MY FATHER + UNCLES NATION-WIDE (LATER DGS) GROCERY STORE AT 13th ST N.W. WE WERE MEMBERS OF OHEV SHALOM AT 5th & I., SHIRLEY POVICH WAS A PROMINENT MEMBER - THE EXHIBIT BRINGS BACK MANY FOND MEMORIES. THANK YOU

Name _BURTON S. EPSTEIN, MD_

Share your memories and stories......

MY GRANDFATHER, SAM HYATT, was one of the few Jewish barbers in the downtown Washington area. He was located for many years near Union Station where people traveled by streetcars to his shop.

Name _ROSALIND FRANKE_

Share your memories and stories......

I was a camper + kitchen helper + counselor @ Kaufmann Camp 1960-1970 + cherish those experiences. Posin's used to give us children a free cookie (!) while our parents shopped. I remember swimming @ the JCC w/out a bathing suit!

Name _Sheldon (or Shelly) Gnatt_

Share your memories and stories......

I am a native Washingtonian and this exhibit is a wonderful tribute to jews of Washington. My paternal great-grandfather was a founding member of Agus Achim and my maternal great-grandfather (and grandfather and uncle) owned/own Alperstein's Furniture. It's so great to be rooted in such a strong community!

Name _rooted in such a strong_
Address/Email _community!_
Thanks so much. - Sandy Levinson

JEWISH WASHINGTON:
SCRAPBOOK OF AN AMERICAN COMMUNITY

Created by the Jewish Historical Society of Greater Washington   Lillian and Albert Small Jewish Museum

Curators
Laura Cohen Apelbaum,
Executive Director
Wendy Turman,
Archivist
Dr. Laura Burd Schiavo

Exhibition Advisor
M. Ann Belkov

Script Writer
Sharon L. Barry

Curatorial Advisors
Dr. Pamela S. Nadell, *Director,
Jewish Studies Program,
American University*
Dr. Hasia Diner, *Paul and Sylvia
Steinberg Professor
of American Jewish History,
New York University*

Exhibition Graphic Design
Jeanne Krohn, Krohn Design

Consulting Exhibition Designers
Gallagher & Associates

Exhibition Fabrication
Infinite Photo and Imaging

Media Production
Spark Media

Special thanks to
Kathryn Schneider Smith,
Cultural Tourism DC and
Annemarie Feld, Feld Design.

The creation of the exhibition was made possible,
in part, by the generous contributions of:

Major Sponsors
Albert and Lillian Small Foundation
Small-Alper Family Foundation

Sponsors
The Jewish Federation of Greater Washington
Barbara & Bert Rein

Monument Club
Andrea Kalin
Jack Kay

Benefactor Club
Blum-Kovler Fund
Dr. Jonathan Grossman
Brenda & Paul Pascal
Ethyl and Shirley Povich Family
Rory & Shelton Zuckerman

Capital Club
United Jewish Endowment Fund
Abramson Family Foundation
Diane & Norman Bernstein
Marshall B. Coyne Foundation
Jonathan S. and Patricia G.
England Family Foundation
Lois & Richard England
Humanities Council of
Washington, D.C.
The Annette M. and Theodore N.
Lerner Family Foundation
Paula Pascal Levine & Family
Joanne & Matthew Tobriner

Potomac Club
Adas Israel Congregation & Melvin
Gelman Religious School
Hannah Aurbach
Ann & Donald Brown
Celebrate 350
Michael Goldstein
Jane & Daniel Solomon
Sprenger Lang Foundation
Samson Stern
Saul Stern
Washington Hebrew Congregation

Columbia Club
Jane Abraham
Wilma & Stuart Bernstein
Martha & Stuart Bindeman
Steve Blacher
Molly & Henry Brylawski
Meg & Sam Flax
Nancy & Carl Gewirz
Marcia & Charles Goldsmith
Shannon & Luchs Insurance
Agency/Jim Hamerski
Nancy Kronheim
Phyllis & Philip Margolius
Bernice & David Stearman

Anniversary Society
Esthy & Jim Adler
Kate Herrod & Richard Alper
Laura & Perry Apelbaum
Flora & Maury Atkin
M. Ann Belkov
Sally Berk
& Sanders H. Berk, MD
Linda & Richard Blumenreich
Fae Brodie
Carol & Morton Brody
Florence K. Brody
E. Fulton Brylawski
Frances & Leonard Burka
Karen & Edward Burka
Maria & Robert Burka
Linda & James Cafritz
Faye & Sheldon S. Cohen
Joy & Robert Cohen
Ryna & Melvin Cohen
Shirley & Joseph Cohen
Alan Dessoff
Joan & Oscar Dodek
Grace & Donald Dody
Margery & Mel Elfin
Nancy Abramowitz & Mark
Ellenberg
Margery & Stuart Elsberg
Nan & Julian Feldman
Rosalie Fonoroff
Carla Freeman
Maryann & Al Friedman
Ann & Frank Gilbert
Rosalie & Joseph Gilbert
Joanne & Norman Goldstein
Sylvia & Harold Greenberg

Sidney Hais*
Tamara & Harry Handelsman
Margot Heckman
Judith & Michael Herman
Sonia & Joseph Herson
Karen & Robert Keats
Marky & Martin Kirsch
Jeannette Kressin
Susan N. & Kenneth J. Luchs
Elaine & Daniel Mann
Carol & John Nannes
Lovell & Jack Olender
Charles Pascal*
Peggy Pearlstein
Muriel F. Rakusin
Jeanne & Lloyd Raport
Sandy & David Reznick
Ellen Sue Shapiro
Clara Schiffer
Theda & Sholom Shefferman
Doris Silverman
Sara & Rabbi Matthew Simon
Roberta & Charles Sonneborn
Joann & Hugh Steinberger
Hadassah N. Thursz
Stephen, Adam & Ben
Trachtenberg in honor of
Francine Trachtenberg
Mendelle Tourover Woodley
Zenith Community Arts
Foundation
* Of blessed memory

Friends
Lucy & Rudolph Arkin
B'nai Tzedek Congregation
Shirley & William Binder
Lenore & George Cohen
Melissa Cohen
Nancy & Edwin Colodny
Sonya & Maurice Dunie
Carolyn Gichner
Sol Gnatt
Lotte Goldman
Paula S. Goldman
Aviva Green
Linda & Jerry Herman
Yetta and Harry Jaffe Family
Cousins Club
Dorothy & Louis Kornhauser
Merrill Lavine
Sarah Pokempner
& Jerry Levine
Linda Lyon
Sandra & Eugene Meyer
Bertha & Saul Mindel
Ruth & David Naftaly
Gerson Nordlinger
Frank Rich, Sr.
Irene Rich
Beverly & Bob Rosen
Dorene & Joseph Rosenthal
Rhea Schwartz
Mildred & Nathan Shankman
Fay Shulman
Lynn & Larry Silverberg
Irving and Esther Strum
Foundation
Pauline & Milton Weinstein
Bunny & Paul Weinstein
Robert Wolff
Sheri & Max Zweig

Exhibition initially mounted in
partnership with the National
Building Museum
Chase Rynd, *Executive Director;*
Martin Mueller, *Senior Vice
President for Special Projects;*
Cathy Crane Frankel, *Director of
Exhibitions;* MaryJane Valade,
*Exhibitions Designer and
Preparator;* Shelagh Cole,
Traveling Exhibitions Manager;
Hank Griffith, *Exhibitions
Coordinator;* Christopher Maclay,
Exhibitions Preparator.

And many thanks to those
who supported the exhibition
with their time, knowledge,
and expertise:
Diana Altman; Helen Belitsky;
Toby Berman; Peter Brownlee;
Lauren Brownstein; Alan Dessoff;
Karen Elkin; Gershon Fishbein;
Patrick Gallagher; Fara Gold;
Janice Goldblum; Diane Goldman;
B. Clarke Green; Rachel Harris;
Dr. Laura Kamoie; Beth Kanter;
Barry Kessler; Glenn Klaus;
Sally Kline; Thomas Lally;
Merrill Lavine; Nathalie Lavine;
Jane Freundel Levey; Rabbi Toby
Manewith; Daniel Mann;
Nelson Marans; Phyllis Myers;
Caren Oberg; Barbara Pappas;
Peggy Pearlstein; Lynn Povich;
Alexis Rice; Lonise Robinson;
Susan Schreiber; Rabbi Amy
Schwartzman; Stephanie
Silverstein; Albert H. Small;
Rebekah Sobel; Charles
Sonneborn; Claire Uziel; Davi
Walders; Carly Ward; Lance Will;
Joel Wind; Rabbi Jeffrey Wohlberg;
Beverly Wolov; Daniel Wolkoff;
and Mendelle Woodley.

Special thanks to
Lois & Richard England
for the accompanying
30-foot banner.

**The exhibition traveled to White Flint
from July 27-November 10, 2006**

The exhibition at White Flint was made possible in part by the following contributors:

Major Supporters
Lerner Enterprises

CARL M. FREEMAN FOUNDATION

Other Supporters
B'nai Israel Congregation
Hebrew Home of Greater Washington

WASHINGTON JEWISH WEEK
Charles E. Smith Jewish Day School
Judah and Molly Greenzaid
Hadassah Greater Washington Area Chapter
Jewish Community Relations Council of Greater Washington
Jewish War Veterans of the USA
Kol Shalom Congregation.

Special thanks to SurroundArt for installation at White Flint.

Accompanying 30-foot banner
made possible through the generosity of Lois & Richard England.

EXHIBITION ACKNOWLEDGMENTS

APPENDIX A

GLOSSARY

Aliyah	Hebrew for "ascent;" refers to one who immigrates to settle in Israel
Aliyah Bet	Clandestine or illegal immigration to Israel
Anschluss	Hitler's annexation of Austria in 1938
Ark	Cabinet in the synagogue storing the Torah scrolls
Ashkenazim	Hebrew for "Germans;" refers to the Jews of Europe, other than those from Spain or Portugal
Bar/Bat Mitzvah	Coming-of-age ceremony for a Jewish boy/girl, traditionally performed when he/she reaches age 13
B'nai B'rith	Founded in 1843, one of the world's oldest and largest Jewish human rights, community action, and humanitarian organizations
Bris (or brit)	Ceremony for ritual circumcision of an 8-day-old male Jewish child
Chazan	Hebrew for "Cantor;" the person who leads the congregation in song and prayer
Cheder	Religious school
Chouchouka	Sephardic appetizer made of tomatoes, garlic, peppers and spices, served with bread or crackers
Dafina	Sephardic stew from Morocco traditionally served for lunch on Shabbat.
Haganah	Jewish underground army in Palestine from the 1920s to the late-1940s
Hanukkah	Eight-day Festival of Lights celebrating religious freedom
Haphtarah	A reading from the Prophets, read along with the weekly Torah (Bible) portion; portion often read by Bar/Bat Mitzvah
Hora	Israeli (circle) dance
Kabalah	Jewish mystical tradition
Kaddish	Memorial prayer
Kashrut	The system of dietary laws that governs whether food is "kosher," or fit to be eaten by observant Jews
Ketubah	Marriage contract
Kibbutz	Cooperative farm in Israel, plural is kibbutzim
K'lal Yisrael	The entire community of Israel
Kosher	Ceremonially clean, according to Jewish law; applied to food, especially to meat of animals slaughtered according to the requirements of Jewish law
Landsman	Fellow countryman
Landsmanschaft	Associations formed by emigrants who came from the same country or hometown in Europe
Magen David	Six-pointed Jewish star (shield) of David, religious marker of Judaism
Menorah	A candelabrum with either seven branches – used in ceremonies to symbolize the seven days of creation – or nine branches – used during the Hanukkah festival
Mezuzah	Small case attached to the doorpost of a house, containing a scroll with passages of scripture; attached to bless the house
Mimouna	A traditionally Sephardic holiday celebrated at the conclusion of Passover, featuring foods such as nuts, honey, and yeast cakes
Minyan	Hebrew for the prayer quorum required for Jewish worship, traditionally consisting of ten males over the age of thirteen
Mohel	One who performs the ritual circumcision
Ner Tamid	Eternal Light hung in front of the Ark in a synagogue
Pogrom	Term of Russian origin referring to anti-Jewish riots in Russia or Europe
Rabbi	Teacher and learned person; spiritual leader of a synagogue
Rosh Hashanah	The Jewish New Year, celebrated on the first and second days of the Hebrew month Tishre in the fall
Seder	Hebrew for "order:" Family home ritual and meal conducted at Passover
Sephardim	Refers to Jews who trace their roots back to the Iberian Peninsula
Shochet	Kosher slaughterer
Shofar	Ram's horn blown as a trumpet during Rosh Hashanah and Yom Kippur
Shul	Yiddish word for synagogue
Sukkah	Booth decorated with fruits and vegetables used during harvest festival of Sukkot
Tallit	Prayer Shawl
Tefillin	Small leather boxes containing Hebrew texts bound to the head and left arm during daily morning prayers
Torah	Hebrew for the first five books of scriptures; traditionally called the Five Books of Moses or Pentateuch; also, a hand-written, rolled, parchment scroll containing the five books of Moses
Tzedakah	Righteousness; obligation to care for others; charity
Yarmulke	Yiddish word for a head covering or skullcap traditionally worn by Jewish men; Hebrew word is kippah
Yiddish	A language used by Jews in or from Central and Eastern Europe, originally a German dialect with words from Hebrew and several modern languages
Yom Kippur	The Day of Atonement, a twenty-five hour fast that climaxes the ten-day period of repentance beginning on Rosh Hashanah
Zionism	Political movement to create and maintain a Jewish state. Derived from Zion, another name for Israel

APPENDIX B

COMMUNITY SCRAPBOOKS

Four scrapbooks in the Jewish Historical Society's archives provide
complementary material about the community's history, documenting a
variety of persons, places, and events. Scrapbook pages include copies
of photographs, correspondence, newsclippings, and other materials
from the Society's archives provided by members of the community.
The scrapbooks are preserved in the Society's archives
and are available for researchers.

Following is a list of subjects included in each of the four scrapbooks.
Scrapbook page numbers follow each entry.

SYNAGOGUES AND COMMUNITY LIFE:
A scrapbook illustrating Jewish communal life
in the Washington area

APPENDIX

APPENDIX C

LIST OF ILLUSTRATIONS

Half a Day on Sunday

Photograph: Isadore Gimble in his grocery, Congress Food Market. JHSGW Collections. Gift of Josephine Gimble. 1993.22. Photograph by Gilbert Gimble.

Photograph: Israel and Lena Lisensky, 1920s. JHSGW Collections. Gift of Gary Malasky. 1996.05

Photograph: Economy Meat Market, 1922. JHSGW Collections. Gift of Mildred and Nathan Shankman. 1996.21

Photograph: DGS store #57. JHSGW Collections.

Photograph: Klivitzky's Kosher Meat and Groceries. JHSGW Collections.

Photograph: Benjamin Dekelbaum in his grocery store, 1925. JHSGW Collections. Gift of Joseph and Rosalie Gilbert. 2004.25

Photograph: Temin family, 1928. JHSGW Collections. Gift of Alvin Temin. 1998.29

Photograph: Morris Silverman's store, 1914. JHSGW Collections. Gift of Robert I. Silverman. 1993.25

On with the Show

Photograph: Palace Theater, 1907. Library of Congress

Photograph: Apex Theater, 1924. Library of Congress

Photograph: Leader Theater, 1910. Library of Congress, Prints and Photographs Division, LOT 12342-10.

Making the Grade

Photograph: Dime Messenger Service, 1912. JHSGW Collections. Gift of Eugene Kressin. 1996.37

Photograph: Jennie Biron, 1917. Gift of Betty Kamerow and Shirley Binder.

Photograph: Temporary war buildings on the Mall, early 1900s. Courtesy of Washingtoniana Division, DC Public Library.

Certificate: Ida Eluto, 1917. JHSGW Collections. Gift of Selma Freedman. 1998.03

Photograph: Hillel Marans, 1918. Courtesy of Nelson Marans.

Synagogue Growth

Photograph: Adas Israel building committee, 1908. ©The Washington Post. Reprinted with permission.

Drawing: Adas Israel exterior, 1908. Courtesy of Adas Israel Congregation.

Minutes: Adas Israel sisterhood. Courtesy of Adas Israel Congregation.

Photograph: Carrie Simon. Courtesy of Washington Hebrew Congregation.

Photograph: Beth Sholom exterior, 1938. Courtesy of Washingtoniana Division, DC Public Library

Photograph: Tifereth Israel choir, 1928. JHSGW Collections. Gift of Louis Kornhauser. 2003.11

Photograph: Washington Hebrew Congregation exterior, 1898. Courtesy of Washingtoniana Division, DC Public Library.

Photograph: Agudath Achim house, 1928. Courtesy of Alexandria Library, Special Collections.

Sketch: Ohev Sholom, 1906. Courtesy of Washingtoniana Division, DC Public Library.

Photograph: Kesher Israel Congregation exterior, 1931. JHSGW Collections.

Photograph: B'nai Israel Congregation and Talmud Torah exterior, 1929. Courtesy of Washingtoniana Division, DC Public Library.

Photograph: Beth El Hebrew Congregation exterior, 1871. Courtesy of Washingtoniana Division, DC Public Library.

Photograph: Talmud Torah exterior, 1906. JHSGW Collections.

The Center of it All

Photograph: Young Women's Hebrew Association dance, 1914. JHSGW Collections. Gift of Janet Kirshner. 1981.03

Photograph: Young Men's Hebrew Association building exterior, 1918. Gift of Jewish Community Center of Greater Washington. 2002.11

Newsletter: "The National Centre," 1925. Gift of Jewish Community Center of Greater Washington. 2002.11

Photographs: various Jewish Community Center images. Gift of Jewish Community Center of Greater Washington. 2002.11

Helping Hands

Program: Kamouflage Karnival. JHSGW Collections.

Photographs: Teachers Rose Lewis (Glaser), Myrtle Cohen, Edith Chidakel (Pascal), Ruth Glazer, and Mary Lewis. JHSGW Collections. Gift of Charles and Edith Chidakel Pascal.

Yearbook: United Hebrew Charities, 1890. JHSGW Collections.

Photograph: Hebrew Home for the Aged, 1914. Courtesy of Hebrew Home of Greater Washington.

Photograph: Jewish Foster Home children, 1908. JHSGW Collections. Gift of Sol Gnatt. 1998.12

Minnie Lansburgh Goldsmith

Card: Minnie Lansburgh Goldsmith. JHSGW Collections. Gift of Patricia England. 1993.19

Photograph: Younger Minnie Lansburgh Goldsmith. JHSGW Collections.

Photograph: Minnie Lansburgh Goldsmith with two women, 1952. ©The Washington Post. Reprinted with permission from the DC Public Library.

Arthur Welsh

Photograph: Arther Welsh with Lieutenant Leighton Hazelhurst, Lieutenant Henry H. (Hap) Arnold, and the Wright C airplane, 1912. JHSGW Collections. Gift of Margaret Smiler Winberg. 1994.61

Photograph: Arthur Welsh in Wright B airplane, 1912. Courtesy of College Park Aviation Museum, Jesse Ayer Collection.

Photograph: Wright C airplane crash, 1912. Courtesy of College Park Aviation Museum, Jesse Ayer Collection.

Shaping the Dream

Card: Daughter of Zion, 1910. JHSGW Collections. Gift of Myrna Goldenberg. 2004.16

Photograph: Poale (Labor) Zion Society, 1917. JHSGW Collections. Gift of Carl Allentuck. 1998.06

Photograph: Orthodox Zionists with President Calvin Coolidge, 1926. JHSGW Collections.

Charity Box. JHSGW Collections. Gift of Judith Bernhardt. 1998.38

1930s-1940s
MEMORIES OF HORROR AND TRIUMPH

Photograph: Gunners, 1944. Washingtoniana Division, DC Public Library.

Great Depression and New Deal

Photographs: Giant store exterior and cashiers, 1936. Courtesy of Giant Food, Inc.

Photograph: Anna Shulman. JHSGW Collections.

Letterhead: Hebrew Sheltering Society, 1931. Courtesy of Roberta Shulman.

Report: Jewish Social Services Agency, 1938. JHSGW Collections. Gift of Jewish Social Service Agency. 1994.07

Photograph: Luna Ereza Diamond, 1945. JHSGW Collections. Gift of Luna Ereza Diamond. 1996.32

Newspaper: Jewish Ledger, 1930. Courtesy of Washington Jewish Week.

Photograph: Joseph Rauh, 1935. ©The Washington Post. Reprinted by permission of Washingtoniana Division, DC Public Library.

Photograph: Clara Goldberg Schiffer, 1935. Gift of Clara Goldberg Schiffer.

Photograph: Robert Nathan, 1933. Library of Congress, Prints & Photographs Division, FSA/OWI Collection, LC-USE6-D-002445.

Photograph: Kronheim delivery van, 1921. JHSGW Collections. Gift of Milton S. Kronheim Estate. 1998.54

Winds of War

Photograph: War Bond Station. Courtesy of Washingtoniana Division, DC Public Library.

Photograph: Rabbi Hugo Schiff, 1939. Courtesy of Beth El Hebrew Congregation.

Photograph: Rabbi Arthur Bogner, 1938. Courtesy of Nathan Bogner.

Photograph: First Lady Eleanor Roosevelt with Frances Gewirz at The Women's Auxiliary of B'nai B'rith Argo Lodge event, 1939. Harris & Ewing Photographs, Courtesy of Carl Gewirz.

Flyer: Mass meeting at Constitution Hall, 1938. Courtesy of American Jewish Historical Society.

Photograph: Scrap metal drive. Courtesy of Washingtoniana Division, DC Public Library.

Jewish Men and Women in Uniform

Photograph: Jewish War Veterans draft pick, 1941. JHSGW Collections. Gift of Dorothy Cooper Kornhauser. 2003.11

Photograph and telegram: Staff Sergeant Morton Brodofsky (Brody), 1945. Courtesy of the Morton Brody family.

Photograph: Fay Shulman, 1945. JHSGW Collections. Gift of Fay Shulman. 2005.6

Photograph: Passover seder at the Willard Hotel, 1942. JHSGW Collections.

Photograph; Major Frank Rich, 1944. Courtesy of Frank Rich.

Photograph: Sidney Hais and Ida Flax Hais, 1942. JHSGW Collections. Gift of Sidney Hais and Steve Blacher. 2002.1

Photograph: Private William Mann, 1944. Courtesy of William Mann.

On the Home Front

Photograph: Army/Navy Award for Gichner Iron Works, 1943. JHSGW Collections. Gift of Isabelle Gichner. 1995.02

Photograph: Agudas Achim Congregation presenting Torah to Marines, 1942. JHSGW Collections.

Flyer: "I am an American Day," 1945. JHSGW Collections.

Photograph: Roselyn Silverman, 1942. Library of Congress. Photograph by Esther Bubley.

Photograph: Phyllis Hagedorn Cohen, 1942. JHSGW Collections. Gift of Phyllis Hagedorn Cohen Fineshriber. 1996.59

Photograph: Fred Kolker with Cantor and *shochet* (ritual butcher) Moshe Yoelson, 1940. Courtesy of Brenda and Paul Pascal.

Photograph: USO dance, 1940s. JHSGW Collections.

Flyer: JCC Youth Rally and Dance, 1942. JHSGW Collections. Gift of Jewish Community Center of Greater Washington. 2002.11

Certificate: Elizabeth C. Hirshman's certificate of recognition for serving as an air raid warden, 1944. JHSGW Collections.

Newspaper: *The District Leader*, 1941. JHSGW Collections. Gift of Bebe Perlmutter. 1995.11

Advertisement: "You Can Help Crush Hitler Now," 1940s. JHSGW Collections. Gift of Bebe Perlmutter. 1995.11

Chaplain Alexander Goode

Photograph and stamps: Chaplain Alexander Goode. JHSGW Collections. Gift of Theresa G. Kaplan. 1995.06

The Dream Continues

Photograph: March of rabbis, 1943. Courtesy of Agudath Israel of America Archives.

Newclipping: Secretary of State Cordell Hull, 1939. ©*The Washington Post*. Reprinted with permission.

Minutes: The Jewish Community Council of Greater Washington, 1942. Courtesy of George Washington University Special Collections.

Photograph: Aaron Goldman. JHSGW Collections. Gift of Aaron Goldman. 1998.41

Photograph: Hymen Goldman. JHSGW Collections. Gift of Aaron Goldman. 1998.41

Flyer: Mass Protest Meeting, 1944.

Photograph: Supreme Court Justice Louis D. Brandeis. JHSGW Collections. Gift of Bernice Kaufmann. 1998.43

Newsclipping: "Zion Officials Installed," 1940. Courtesy of *Washington Jewish Week*.

Program: "We Will Never Die," 1943. JHSGW Collections. Gift of Harry Selden. 1998.44

Saving the Children

Pledge Card: "My Pledge for Youth Aliyah." JHSGW Collections. Gift of James Cafritz. 1995.12

Photograph: Denise Tourover, Courtesy of *Washington Jewish Week*.

Letter: Elinor Morgenthau, 1943. Courtesy of Hadassah: Women's Zionist Organization of America.

Photograph: Sally Kravette, 1947. Courtesy of Sally Kravette.

Flyer: "Mrs. Edward Cafritz Broadcast on Youth Aliyah'," 1945. JHSGW Collections. Gift of James Cafritz. 1995.12

Relief and Rescue After the War

Photograph: Giv'at Washington, 1946. JHSGW Collections. Gift of Aviva Green. 1998.35

Photograph: Elinor Morgenthau, 1943. Courtesy of Hadassah: Women's Zionist Organization of America.

Photograph: Rabbi Zemach Green. JHSGW Collections. Gift of Aviva Green. 1998.35

Advertisements: United Jewish Appeal, 1946-1948. Courtesy of Washington Jewish Week.

Photograph: S.S. *Ben Hecht*, 1946. JHSGW Collections. Gift of Harry Selden. 1998.44

Photograph: Elihu Bergman. JHSGW Collections. Gift of Elihu Bergman.1998.68

Securing the Dream

Photograph: Habonim march, 1946. JHSGW Collections. Gift of Carl Allentuck. 1998.06

Photograph: Dr. Harvey Ammerman. Courtesy of Dr. Bruce Ammerman

S.S. *Exodus 1947* protest, 1947. JHSGW Collections.

Letter: Edmund I. Kaufmann, 1945. JHSGW Collections. Gift of Bernice Kaufmann. 1998.43

Tally sheet: United Nations vote, 1947. Courtesy of Sylvia Turover Sittenfeld and Ruthe Turover Katz.

Photograph: Jacob Kamerow. JHSGW Collections. Gift of Martin Kamerow. 1998.46

Photograph: Joseph Cherner. Courtesy of Rickey Cherner.

Photograph: Abraham Kay. JHSGW Collections. Gift of Jack Kay. 1998.48

Photograph: Ruth Cherner. Courtesy of Rickey Cherner.

Photograph: Isador Turover. JHSGW Collections.

Photograph: Leo Bernstein. Courtesy of Leo Bernstein.

Photograph: Morris Pollin. JHSGW Collections.

Photograph: Theodore Herzl Levin. Courtesy of Barbara Levin.

Photograph: Morris Rodman. JHSGW Collections. Gift of Betsy Salandria. 1992.02

Photograph: Hymen Goldman. JHSGW Collections. Gfit of Aaron Goldman. 1998.41

A Dream Comes True

Photograph: Flag-raising, 1948. ©*The Washington Post*. Reprinted with permission.

Photograph: Habonim *hora*, 1948. JHSGW Collections. Gift of Judith Bernhardt. 1998.38

Building a Nation

Photograph: Abraham S. Kay and Prime Minister David Ben-Gurion, 1950. JHSGW Collections. Gift of Jack Kay. 1998.48

Photograph: Naharia convalescent home. JHSGW Collections. Gift of Jack Kay. 1998.48

Photograph: Dorothy and Jack Bender, Naomi and Nehemiah Cohen, and Minnie and Abraham Kay, 1950s. JHSGW Collections. Gift of Jack Kay. 1998.48

Photograph: Nehemiah Cohen and David Ben-Gurion, 1950s. Courtesy of Daniel Solomon.

Photograph: Zionist Organization of America packaging canned goods, 1948. Courtesy of Arnold and Sally Kravette.

Photograph: Celia Grossberg, 1956. JHSGW Collections. Gift of Perla Fox. 1998.76

Photograph: Carl, Doris, and Leba Allentuck, 1949. Courtesy of Eliot J. Allentuck.

Restrictions

Photograph: Beverly Beach Club, 1950s. Courtesy of Maryland State Archives.

Photograph: Albert Arent. Courtesy of Albert Arent.

1950s-1980s
SPREADING OUT

Photograph: Fred Goldberg and Paula Pascal, 1955. JHSGW Collections. Gift of Paula Pascal Levine. 2001.06

Photograph: Kemp Mill Estates. Courtesy of Jack Kay.

Mom & Pop No More (1)

Photograph: Stern Office Furniture, Inc. and Sam & Saul Stern, 1966. JHSGW Collections. Gift of Sam, Saul, Andrew, and Eve Stern. 2003.25

Brochure: "Kann's Virginia," 1951. Courtesy of Bernei Burgunder.

Shopping Bag: G Street Remnant Shop. Courtesy of G Street Fabrics

Mom & Pop No More (2)

Photograph and advertisement: Jumbo, 1950s. Courtesy of Karen Herman Keats.

Photograph: Giant exterior, 1959. Courtesy of Giant Food, Inc.

Photograph: N.M. Cohen & Samuel Lehrman. Courtesy of Giant Food, Inc. and the family of Charlotte and Jacob (Jac) Lehrman

Photograph: Drug Fair, 1960. JHSGW Collections. Gift of Stuart Elsberg. 1998.20

Photograph: Hechinger Company exterior, 1957. Courtesy of the Historical Society of Washington.

Photograph: Hechinger ribbon-cutting, 1961. Courtesy of the Historical Society of Washington.

Mom & Pop No More (3)

Photograph: Marlo's exterior, 1963. ©*Washington Post*; reprinted by permission of the DC Public Library.

Photograph: Marlo's interior, 1972. ©*Washington Post*; reprinted by permission of the DC Public Library.

Photograph: Rosenthal Chevrolet groundbreaking, 1954. Courtesy of Robert Rosenthal.

Photograph: Pasternak's window display, 1953. JHSGW Collections. Gift of Alfred Pasternak. 1984.06

Photograph: Morton's, 1980s. JHSGW Collections.

Poster: "Stay out of Hecht's," 1951. Courtesy of Bennett Caplan.

Shopping Bag: G Street Fabrics. Courtesy of G Street Fabrics.

Washington's Sephardic Community

Photograph: Yom Tov Congregation, 1936. JHSGW Collections. Gift of Luna Diamond. 1996.32

Photograph: Albert and Stella Emsellem, 1950s. Courtesy of Irene Kaplan.

Photographs: Magen David exterior and interior, 1998. Courtesy of Magen David Sephardic Congregation.

Real Estate Boom

Photograph: Beltway opening, 1964. ©*Washington Post*; reprinted by permission of the DC Public Library.

Photograph: Universal South at 1825 Connecticut Avenue, NW, 1959. Courtesy of The Cafritz Company.

Lease: Kaywood Gardens. JHSGW Collections. Gift of Joseph and Rosalie Gilbert. 2004. 25

Newsletter: Indian Spring Country Club, 1954. JHSGW Collections. Gift of Jack Kay. 2000.19

Photograph: Kemp Mill Estates, 1950s. Courtesy of Jack Kay.

Photograph: Washingtonian Towers, 1965. Courtesy of Montgomery County Historical Society.

Photograph: Silver Spring Shopping Center, 1938. Courtesy of Montgomery County Historical Society.

Photograph: Somerset House, 2000. Courtesy of Albert H. Small.

Brochure: Americana Apartments, 1950s. Courtesy of Carl M. Freeman Companies.

Photograph: Wheaton Plaza, 1959. Courtesy of Montgomery County Historical Society.

Photograph: Crystal City, 1960s. Courtesy of Bernard Gewirz.

Photograph: Montgomery Building, 1968. Courtesy of Bernard Gewirz.

Photograph: Shannon & Luchs. Courtesy of Kenneth Luchs.

New Synagogues

Photograph: C. Edward Goldberg, congregation president, speaking at the Arlington Fairfax Jewish Center groundbreaking, 1948. Courtesy of Leslie Goldberg.

Brochure: Montgomery County Jewish Community, 1947. JHSGW Collections. Gift of Rabbi Tzvi and Esther Porath. 2003.15

Photograph: President Dwight D. Eisenhower at Washington Hebrew Congregation, 1955. Courtesy of Washington Hebrew Congregation.

Photograph: Talmud Torah destruction, 1959. ©*Washington Post*; reprinted by permission of the DC Public Library.

Photograph: Temple Sinai cornerstone-laying, 1956. Courtesy of Temple Sinai.

Newsletter: *The Jewish Star*, 1957. JHSGW Collections. Gift of Bebe Perlmutter. 1995.11

Brochure: Congregation Shaare Tikvah, 1965. JHSGW Collections. Gift of Bebe Perlmutter. 1995.11

Photograph: Temple Micah exterior, 1960s. Courtesy of Temple Micah.

Expanding in All Directions

Map, 1956. JHSGW Collections. Gift of Aaron Goldman. 1998.41

Photograph: Charles E. Smith at Rockville campus groundbreaking, 1968. ©*Washington Post*; reprinted by permission of the DC Public Library.

Photograph: Jewish Community Center of Northern Virginia, 1990. Courtesy of Jewish Community Center of Northern Virginia.

Photograph: Virginia Governor Douglas Wilder attaching *mezuzah*, 1991. Courtesy of Jewish Community Center of Northern Virginia.

Photograph: Miriam Bazelon, 1959. JHSGW Collections. Gift of Jewish Social Service Agency. 1998.02

Report: United Jewish Appeal Honor Roll, 1959. JHSGW Collections. Gift of Daniel Thursz. 2001.15

Photograph: United Jewish Appeal local leaders, 1964. JHSGW Collections.

Flyer: United Jewish Appeal Government Division, 1965. JHSGW Collections. Gift of The Jewish Federation of Greater Washington. 2004.14

Advertisement: Super Sunday, 1976. JHSGW Collections. Gift of Ruth White. 2002.19

Jewish Activism

Photograph: Protestors at Lafayette Park, 1967. JHSGW Collections. Photograph by Ida Jervis. Gift of Ida Jervis. 1998.58

Photograph: Neighbors Inc. event, 1958. Courtesy of Bennett Caplan.

Photograph: Glen Echo picketing, 1960. Courtesy of Hyman Bookbinder.

Photograph: Police checking Rabbi Emmet Frank's car, 1958. Courtesy of Beth El Hebrew Congregation.

Magazine: *United Synagogue Review*, 1964. JHSGW Collections. Gift of Bebe Perlmutter. 1995.11

Photograph: Soviet Embassy vigil. Courtesy of National Conference for Soviet Jewry.

Photograph: Vigil at Lincoln Memorial, 1971. JHSGW Collections. Photograph by Ida Jervis. Gift of Ida Jervis. 1998.58

Newspaper: *Washington Jewish Week*, 1987. JHSGW Collections. Gift of Bebe Perlmutter. 1995.11

Photograph: Isaac Franck dancing the *hora* with Mayor Walter Washington, 1973. JHSGW Collections. Gift of Pearl Franck. 1999.13

Marching for Jobs and Freedom

Photograph: March on Washington, 1963. JHSGW Collections. Gift of Pearl Franck. 1993.13

National and International Arena

Photograph: Dr. Seymour and Cecile Alpert, Israeli Ambassador Avraham and Zena Harman, and Morris and Jennie Pollin. JHSGW Collections. Gift of Seymour Alpert. 2005.11

Photograph: Rabbi Stanley Rabinowitz, Ambassador Yitzhak Rabin, Prime Minister Golda Meir, and Simcha Dinitz, 1969. Courtesy of Adas Israel Congregation. Photograph by Mel Chamowitz.

Photograph: Ambassador Yitzhak Rabin, Conductor Zubin Mehta, Norman Bernstein, and David Lloyd Kreeger, 1971. Courtesy of Norman Bernstein.

Report: *Near East Report*, 1967. JHSGW Collections. Gift of Ruth White. 2002.19

Photograph: Participants in the March on Washington, 1963. Courtesy of Religious Action Center of Reform Judaism.

Magazine: *The National Jewish Monthly*, 1977. JHSGW Collections. Gift of Hadassah Thursz. 2001.15

Program: Union of Orthodox Jewish Congregations of America convention, 1964. JHSGW Collections. Gift of Bebe Perlmutter. 1995.11

Report: National ZOA Convention Report, 1980. JHSGW Collections. Gift of Bebe Perlmutter. 1995.11

Government Service

Photograph: Sheldon S. Cohen and President Lyndon B. Johnson, 1968. Courtesy of Sheldon S. Cohen.

Photograph: Joseph B. Gildenhorn with President George Bush, 1990. Courtesy of Joseph B. Gildenhorn.

Photograph: Stuart Eizenstat, with President Jimmy Carter, 1977. Courtesy of Stuart Eizenstat.

Photograph: Ann Brown with Vice President Al Gore, 1994. Courtesy of Ann Brown.

Photograph: Ambassador Stuart Bernstein, 2001. Courtesy of Stuart Bernstein.

Photograph: Nettie Ottenberg in carriage, 1964. ©*Washington Post*; reprinted by permission of the DC Public Library.

Photograph: President John F. Kennedy, President of Brazil João Goulart, and D.C. Board of Commissioners Chairman Walter N. Tobriner, 1962. JHSGW Collections. Gift of Constance Povich. 2004.13

Photograph: John Hechinger, Sr. and Gilbert Hahn, Jr., 1969. ©*Washington Post*; reprinted by permission of the DC Public Library.

APPENDIX D

INDEX